Mary Shelley: A Very Short Introduction

VERY SHORT INTRODUCTIONS are for anyone wanting a stimulating and accessible way into a new subject. They are written by experts, and have been translated into more than 45 different languages.

The series began in 1995, and now covers a wide variety of topics in every discipline. The VSI library currently contains over 700 volumes—a Very Short Introduction to everything from Psychology and Philosophy of Science to American History and Relativity—and continues to grow in every subject area.

Very Short Introductions available now:

ABOLITIONISM Richard S. Newman
THE ABRAHAMIC RELIGIONS
    Charles L. Cohen
ACCOUNTING Christopher Nobes
ADOLESCENCE Peter K. Smith
THEODOR W. ADORNO
    Andrew Bowie
ADVERTISING Winston Fletcher
AERIAL WARFARE Frank Ledwidge
AESTHETICS Bence Nanay
AFRICAN AMERICAN RELIGION
    Eddie S. Glaude Jr
AFRICAN HISTORY John Parker and
    Richard Rathbone
AFRICAN POLITICS Ian Taylor
AFRICAN RELIGIONS Jacob K. Olupona
AGEING Nancy A. Pachana
AGNOSTICISM Robin Le Poidevin
AGRICULTURE Paul Brassley and
    Richard Soffe
ALEXANDER THE GREAT
    Hugh Bowden
ALGEBRA Peter M. Higgins
AMERICAN BUSINESS HISTORY
    Walter A. Friedman
AMERICAN CULTURAL HISTORY
    Eric Avila
AMERICAN FOREIGN RELATIONS
    Andrew Preston
AMERICAN HISTORY Paul S. Boyer
AMERICAN IMMIGRATION
    David A. Gerber
AMERICAN INTELLECTUAL
    HISTORY
    Jennifer Ratner-Rosenhagen

AMERICAN LEGAL
    HISTORY G. Edward White
AMERICAN MILITARY HISTORY
    Joseph T. Glatthaar
AMERICAN NAVAL HISTORY
    Craig L. Symonds
AMERICAN POETRY David Caplan
AMERICAN POLITICAL HISTORY
    Donald Critchlow
AMERICAN POLITICAL PARTIES
    AND ELECTIONS L. Sandy Maisel
AMERICAN POLITICS
    Richard M. Valelly
THE AMERICAN PRESIDENCY
    Charles O. Jones
THE AMERICAN REVOLUTION
    Robert J. Allison
AMERICAN SLAVERY
    Heather Andrea Williams
THE AMERICAN SOUTH
    Charles Reagan Wilson
THE AMERICAN WEST
    Stephen Aron
AMERICAN WOMEN'S HISTORY
    Susan Ware
AMPHIBIANS T. S. Kemp
ANAESTHESIA Aidan O'Donnell
ANALYTIC PHILOSOPHY
    Michael Beaney
ANARCHISM Colin Ward
ANCIENT ASSYRIA Karen Radner
ANCIENT EGYPT Ian Shaw
ANCIENT EGYPTIAN ART AND
    ARCHITECTURE Christina Riggs
ANCIENT GREECE Paul Cartledge

Available soon:

For more information visit our website

www.oup.com/vsi/

Charlotte Gordon

MARY SHELLEY

A Very Short Introduction

OXFORD
UNIVERSITY PRESS

OXFORD

UNIVERSITY PRESS

Great Clarendon Street, Oxford, OX2 6DP,
United Kingdom

Oxford University Press is a department of the University of Oxford.
It furthers the University's objective of excellence in research, scholarship,
and education by publishing worldwide. Oxford is a registered trade mark of
Oxford University Press in the UK and in certain other countries

Published in the United States of America by Oxford University Press
198 Madison Avenue, New York, NY 10016, United States of America

British Library Cataloguing in Publication Data

Data available

Library of Congress Control Number: 2021948696

ISBN 978–0–19–886919–1

Printed in Great Britain by
Ashford Colour Press Ltd, Gosport, Hampshire

To G.W., dear friend, fearless editor

Contents

Acknowledgements

I would like to thank Gabrielle Watling, Ph.D. for her expert assistance in preparing this manuscript. I am also grateful to Endicott College for support during the writing process.

List of illustrations

Chapter 1
Legacies

Mary Shelley: author of *Frankenstein*

This is all that most people know about Mary Shelley. If they know anything else, they might also know her as the 16-year-old girl who ran away with poet Percy Shelley.

But Mary Shelley was far more than a one-book author, and far more than the young woman who loved Percy. She outlived Percy by almost 30 years, publishing eight more books after *Frankenstein* and more than 50 short stories and essays. She wrote biographical sketches and introduced Percy's work to the reading public, editing and compiling his poetry and prose. The mystery is why most people only know her for the first book she wrote, particularly as it was published when she was only 19 years old. Taken as a whole, her work represents a remarkable commitment to social reform and women's independence. Stylistically, she broke conventions and stretched 19th-century literary genres to accommodate the themes and ideas she wanted to express. She published novels set in her own time, historical novels, and a dystopian futuristic novel that is eerily predictive of the calamities that we face today. Her stories and essays were experimental, insightful, and fascinating. Her life, too, was remarkable for its creativity and courage. She set her own rules, supporting herself and her family and friends with her writing for most of her adult life. She broke with convention by bearing children out of wedlock. She travelled throughout Europe, and lived as an independent woman during a time when middle-class women were supposed to be wives and mothers, not famous authors.

But neglect and misunderstanding are an essential part of the Mary Shelley story. Her reputation suffered after her death, for political reasons but also because of the history of women and women writers. For over a century, she was overshadowed by her famous husband. Only recently have her complete works been deemed worthy of study. She has been the subject of many biographies, but, unfortunately, some of these perpetuated the falsehoods surrounding her life story, as her enemies did their best to destroy her reputation and her loved ones tried to conceal the truths they considered too scandalous for public consumption. Any study of Mary Shelley must address the dilemma of how much of her life should be included in a study of her literary achievements. There is no easy answer to this dilemma, but neither is it an either/or construction. Although it is important to read Mary Shelley's works as stand-alone texts, her literary and personal choices did not happen in the abstract. She based many of her decisions on the ideas of her parents, the authors Mary Wollstonecraft and William Godwin. As she grew older, her relationship with Percy would also shape her life as a woman and a writer. Mary Shelley's life was a creative enterprise. She inscribed her choices in time, the way she inscribed words in her notebook. Accordingly, in this book, her biography and her literary texts will be studied side by side in order to reveal how her life informs her work. In addition, she will be referred to as Mary Shelley throughout, even though she was born Mary Godwin. This is to rectify the past practice of referring to her husband as Shelley, and Mary by her first name, a diminishment of her status as an author.

Legacy

Mary Shelley's birthday, 30 August 1797, marks both a beginning and an end, the start of one life and the close of another (Figure 1). When she was born, she was so weak that it seemed likely she would die within a few days. Her mother, the political philosopher Mary Wollstonecraft, author of *A Vindication of the Rights of Woman*, who had already given birth to a sturdy little girl three years earlier, reassured her husband, William Godwin, that the infant would thrive, and devoted herself to strengthening the child, delighting in her new daughter. Unfortunately, tragedy struck a few days later. Wollstonecraft began to shake and sweat with childbed fever. Her daughter was taken from her arms and Wollstonecraft died, 11 days after giving birth—a shocking loss for

1. William Godwin's diary entry, noting the birth of Mary Shelley. 'Birth of Mary, 20 minutes after 11 at night' (fourth entry down).

the world, but, most of all, for the little girl who would never have a mother.

Wollstonecraft's death played a decisive role in Mary Shelley's life and in her development as a writer. Haunted by the thought of the mother she never knew, she dedicated herself to upholding Wollstonecraft's progressive principles, devoting much of her work to advocating for women and social reform, using changing literary strategies. In *Frankenstein*, she depicted a dystopian world, where the female characters are unable to counter Victor Frankenstein's ambitions and the results are catastrophic. In her seventh and final novel, *Falkner*, the female characters are wise, capable, and effective; they persuade the male characters to abandon their destructive impulses and create a utopian society of domestic tranquillity. In her non-fiction she also argued on behalf of women. In the biographical articles on prominent male authors that she wrote for Dionysius Lardner's *Cabinet Cyclopaedia*, an encyclopedia organized into nine 'cabinets' or areas (instead of the alphabetical organization of the *Encyclopaedia Britannica*) which appeared between 1829 and 1846, she made sure to include the women in the men's lives, depicting their wives, sisters, daughters, mothers, and lovers. In her short fiction, she also emphasized the importance of women, depicting the dangers of male tyranny and female passivity. In her travelogues, she asserted her right as a woman author to have her own opinions on politics, art, education, and history. In all of her work, she made her point clear: if women were allowed greater independence, if they had more power in the world, there would be less violence, greater equity, and less injustice. Improving the rights of women would improve the world; social reform was essential for all of humanity.

She applied these principles to her own life, asserting her right to independence by flouting the conventions that restricted the behaviour of young women. She also helped women friends escape oppressive marriages and gave what money she could to women who needed financial support. And yet, despite her radical ideas and rule-breaking behaviour, despite her lifelong commitment to advancing Wollstonecraft's causes—the rights of women, social justice, and educational and political reform—for more than a century after her death, scholars described her as fearful, conservative and, even, a hypocrite. In part, this was because her daughter-in-law, Jane Shelley, tried to make Mary Shelley acceptable to the conservative Victorian public by hiding her mother-in-law's scandal-ridden past, burning her letters and ripping pages from her diaries. Obituary writers followed suit, painting Mary Shelley as an ideal Victorian wife and minimizing her literary achievements: 'It is not as the authoress even of *Frankenstein* that she derives her most enduring and endearing title to our affection,' read Mary Shelley's death notice in *The Literary Gazette*, 'but as the faithful and devoted wife of Percy Bysshe Shelley.'

The absurdity of this appraisal would not have been lost on Mary Shelley who, 37 years earlier, had been castigated for running away with Percy and bearing children out of wedlock. To Mary Shelley, what would have caused true pain was the faint praise for her literary work, particularly the failure to mention the five other novels she had published after *Frankenstein*, her short stories, travelogues, essays, and her many articles. But for the Victorian reading public, a woman could earn no higher praise than being termed a good wife; the erasure of Mary Shelley's literary contributions and the elevation of her role as a 'wife' represented a triumph for her daughter-in-law. Her enemies leapt upon this mischaracterization and the consequences were severe, as Mary Shelley's stature as a bold, innovative writer was almost lost to history.

Critical appraisal of Mary Shelley

Mary Shelley may not have realized the extent to which she contributed to her own problematic reputation. After Percy's premature death at the age of 29, she devoted herself to building his fame as a poet, painting herself out of the picture, making no mention of the significant role she played in editing his papers, which he had left in such profound disarray that she had to reconstitute poems he had scrawled on different scraps of paper, or on the backs of letters or stories—a Herculean effort. In her biographical notes, she depicted him as a selfless artist, a martyr for the cause of literature, and described herself as an admiring acolyte, leaving out any discussion of their shared reading, her role as a commentator on his work, and her own work as a writer. She was also silent about his atheism and only hinted at his political activism, both of which would have shocked Victorian readers and antagonized Percy's conservative father, who could block the publication of Percy's poetry whenever he wanted. As she explained to the reader in her preface to Percy's collected works (1839), what mattered was Percy's poetry, and the poet's 'exalted nature'. Later, in less conservative times, she implied, the whole truth could be told. Her efforts worked, but with unforeseen consequences. Not only had she created a literary character named 'Percy Shelley', an angelic otherworldly poet, who bore little resemblance to the actual Percy she had lived with for years, she had also created another character, 'Mary Shelley', a selfless and devoted wife. As 'Percy Shelley's' fame grew, so did 'Mary Shelley's' with the result that she became known primarily as Percy's wife, rather than an author in her own right, even though, in 1830, she was named the most distinguished woman writer of the era by the notable literary magazine *The Athenaeum*.

When she died, her friends and enemies fought over who she had really been. Her daughter-in-law's efforts to make her more palatable to the prim Victorian audience exacerbated the problem. Edward Trelawny, an adventurer and writer, who had known Percy for less than a year, downplayed the importance of Mary Shelley in order to cast himself as the central character in Percy's life. In Trelawny's version of events, he was the only person worthy of writing Percy's life, as Mary Shelley was a hypocrite, a prig, and unworthy of Percy's love.

Unfortunately, many literary critics of the 20th century followed Trelawny's lead, accepting his memoir as truth, and discounting Mary's own radical principles, her innovations as a writer, and her commitment to social change. There were exceptions, of course. In 1951, in a ground-breaking biography, Muriel Spark reappraised Mary Shelley, drawing attention to her sophistication as a novelist and her rebellious nature. But Spark's was a lone voice. Even in the 1970s, when there was a new interest in the work of historical women, many scholars continued to echo Trelawny's falsehoods. In 1974, Richard Holmes, Percy Shelley's biographer, made the unfortunate claim that Mary was a lesser literary light and an unworthy wife to Percy (a stance for which he has since apologized). The scholar Betty T. Bennett wrote that when she published the first volume of Mary Shelley's letters in 1980 one reviewer 'suggested that Mary Shelley's letters were not worth publishing'. Those critics who did pay attention to Shelley's literary achievements tended to focus exclusively on *Frankenstein*, at the expense of her other writing. Feminist scholars of the 1970s and 1980s interpreted her work as growing more conservative over time, expressing their disappointment in what they regarded as a retreat from the public sphere.

Over the last 30 years, the critical tide has turned. Undeterred by the historical dismissal of Mary Shelley, recent biographers and literary scholars have devoted their careers to analysing her writing, revealing the innovations of her lesser-known novels, her short stories, her travel writing, and her biographical essays. Biographers have combed through archives, discovering new documents that illuminate Mary Shelley's self-discipline as a professional writer, her originality as a novelist, her devotion to radical causes, and her seriousness as a political thinker.

As a result, Mary Shelley's importance as a writer and as an advocate for social reform is now well established. Conferences are devoted to the study of her work and her life. And yet, hers is a cautionary tale, for the true Mary Shelley almost vanished from the records, despite the fact that her principles were always there for everyone to see. In her work, she repeatedly announced her allegiance to her mother's philosophy by emphasizing the importance of female friendship, women's independence, the primacy of education, and the dangerous consequences of unchecked male ambition. Her dedication to exploring and prioritizing women's experience led her to overturn literary conventions, expanding the parameters of the historical and Gothic novel, and experimenting with literary strategies and style. Recent biographers have shown that she used what power she had to fight for women's independence, helping her friends escape abusive fathers and husbands and giving money to women in need. In the privacy of her journal, she wrote, 'I have ever defended women when oppressed.'

At no point did she seek to hide her dedication to her mother's ideals. Indeed, she emphasized the role her mother played in her life, frequently expressing her admiration. In a letter to her friend Frances Wright, she wrote:

> The memory of my Mother has always been the pride and delight of my life & the admiration of others for her, has been the cause of most of the happiness...I have enjoyed. Her greatness of soul [has] perpetually reminded me that I ought to degenerate as little as I could from those from who I derived my being.

In 1831, in a preface for a new edition of her father's novel *Caleb Williams*, she declared:

> The writings of this celebrated woman are monuments of her moral and intellectual superiority. Her lofty spirit, her eager assertion of the claims of her sex, animate the 'Vindication of the Rights of Woman'....Her unwearied exertions for the benefit of others, her rectitude, her independence, joined to a warm affectionate heart and the most refined softness of manners, made her the idol of all who knew her.

And yet, despite Mary Shelley's public statements, despite the breadth and depth of her literary innovations, and her advocacy for women's independence in her fiction, until recently most readers did not grasp the extent of Wollstonecraft's impact on her daughter, an oversight which stems from and has contributed to the misunderstanding of Mary Shelley's life and work. Those critics who saw Mary Shelley as a conservative, or, worse, as a hypocrite, depicted mother and daughter as opposites, painting Wollstonecraft as a social reformer and Mary Shelley as a compromiser. This depiction of Mary Shelley was compounded by the different literary strategies deployed by mother and daughter. Mary Shelley expressed many of her most radical ideas through the voices and actions of fictional characters, while Wollstonecraft explicitly outlined her beliefs in her essays; even in her novels, Wollstonecraft's style was emphatic and argumentative, ensuring that readers understood her points, whereas Mary Shelley's fiction was multifaceted, containing competing points of view. Biographers also played a role, with many assuming that Wollstonecraft had a limited influence on her daughter's work since she died immediately after her birth. They also point to the fact that Wollstonecraft lived during more radical times. Aged 16 when the American Revolution broke out, Wollstonecraft lived and worked during the progressive era of the Enlightenment and helped promote the early ideals of Romanticism. Mary Shelley, on the other hand, began her life during the Romantic era, but ended her years in the repressive atmosphere of the mid-19th century.

But, understanding Wollstonecraft's legacy is the key to understanding her daughter, as, over the course of her long writing career, Mary Shelley strove to live up to her mother's radical philosophy and dedicated her life to fulfilling her mother's dreams. Far from becoming more conservative as a writer, she grew increasingly radical, exposing the harm done by allowing men too much power and women too little. In her final novels, the female characters are strong enough to create what the critic Ann

Mellor calls 'the egalitarian bourgeois family' and another describes as 'utopian domesticity', triumphing over the traditional male values of war, honour, and individual ambition.

Mary Wollstonecraft

Famous today for advocating for the rights of women in her *Vindication of the Rights of Woman*, Mary Wollstonecraft also published *A Vindication of the Rights of Men*, a fiery attack on tyranny in all its various forms—legal, economic, social, religious, and political. An outspoken advocate for change, Mary Wollstonecraft (Figure 2) denounced the unfair laws and prejudices that oppressed all human beings. She supported the French and Haitian revolutions of the late 18th century, the anti-slavery movement, and social reform. In all of her work, she argued on behalf of what she termed 'the rights of humanity', fighting against the exploitation of working-class people, children, women, Native Americans, and enslaved people.

Hated by her enemies and revered by her supporters, Wollstonecraft believed that educational reform was the best way for individuals to gain greater liberty. All people were entitled to direct their own lives, including women, she argued, an idea foreign to those experts who preached that females were incapable of thinking for themselves. If women had too much freedom, these experts held, they would disrupt the 'natural' order of society; women were weaker than men, had smaller brains, and were easily misled. They should be kept safely at home, where they could be protected by the men in their lives—upper- and middle-class women, that is. Few people thought about protecting working-class women, who were routinely subjected to abuse and violence—a situation that outraged Wollstonecraft, and which she addressed in her final, unfinished novel, *Maria, or the Wrongs of Woman*. In this work of fiction, Jemima, a maid, details the rape and abuse she undergoes at the hands of her employer.

2. **Mary Wollstonecraft, pregnant with Mary Shelley, by John Opie (1797).**

Wollstonecraft has Jemima tell her story in her own voice, one of the first times that a working-class woman is put centre stage in English fiction. Jemima tells her story to a young middle-class wife, Maria, who outlines her own sad story of abuse: she has been thrown into an asylum by her tyrannical husband, who has seized their child as his lawful 'property'. 'Is not the world a vast prison,' Maria asks, 'and women born slaves?'

11

By giving equal weight to the voices of both women, Wollstonecraft underlined the point that all women were vulnerable to abuse. Working-class and poor women were subject to the abuse of their employers. But wealth was no protection. Middle-class women were 'sold' by their fathers to husbands they did not love, in exchange for financial settlements. Once they were married, they had to surrender their rights to their husbands. In the English system of coverture, husbands assumed control of their wives' legal, economic, religious, and political identities. Accordingly, wives could not own property, vote, represent themselves in the legal system, or even attend the church of their choice; children were considered the property of their fathers. Wives did not gain the right to own property until 1870, with the passage of the Married Women's Property Act, and could not vote until 1928. To most 18th-century English people, women's rights seemed as absurd as the rights of animals. In fact, animals would gain legal protection before women. (In 1824, 20 years before the first law was passed that limited, but did not prohibit, violence against women, a law was passed that prohibited the abuse of animals.)

Wollstonecraft did not hide the fact that she wanted to overturn this system. She wanted women to be able to live independent lives, not just for their own sakes, but for the sake of all humanity. In a *Vindication of the Rights of Woman*, she argued that men's lives would improve if women were allowed their freedom. But this was sacrilege to conservatives, who declared her a threat to society. They believed that if young women read her work, they would be corrupted by her philosophy, and launched a public vendetta against her led by Horace Walpole, who called her 'a hyena in petticoats' and 'a whore'. So successful was their campaign that if you looked up 'Prostitution' in the index of the influential newspaper *The Anti-Jacobin Review*, it said, 'See Mary Wollstonecraft.' But despite these attacks, Wollstonecraft continued to argue for justice, publishing her ideas in books and articles, translations and reviews, one of the first English women to earn her living as a writer.

Mary Wollstonecraft and William Godwin

Wollstonecraft's commitment to radical principles was supported by her husband, the author William Godwin, another prominent advocate for social reform. United in their belief that every human being was entitled to freedom, Wollstonecraft and Godwin formed a powerful union, joining forces to fight for change. In his monumental work *An Enquiry Concerning Political Justice, and Its Influence on General Virtue and Happiness* (1793), Godwin declared that all governments, not only unjust ones, infringed the natural rights of the individual. Known today as the father of anarchy, he argued that human beings should be allowed to govern themselves and that governments restricted the liberty of their citizens. He argued that it was reason, and reason alone, that could save human beings from themselves—a moderate stance that was lost on most of his readers. To them, the sheer shock value of *Political Justice* transformed Godwin into an icon of revolution. Radicals of all stripes celebrated him as their hero, including, 20 years later, the young poet Percy Shelley.

Although Godwin and Wollstonecraft loved one another, they resisted getting married. Both believed that marriage was an institution that debased women, and they were right. Not only did the law of coverture restrict the rights of wives, it was against the law for any woman to escape from an abusive father, husband, or brother. No wife could initiate divorce. Men were held responsible for their wives' behaviour and were encouraged to 'discipline' them if they became unruly. If a husband failed to enforce his will, allowing his wife to get out hand, he was publicly shunned, his masculinity called into question. He could even face legal challenges. Those few women who did try to flee a cruel husband were considered outlaws since a man had the legal right to pursue his wife and imprison her or commit her to an institution, as Wollstonecraft had depicted in *Maria*.

For almost a year, they conducted their affair in secret, but in 1797, when Wollstonecraft discovered she was pregnant, they faced a dilemma. Women who bore children out of wedlock were punished with social exile, as were their children. Wollstonecraft had already faced this situation. During the French Revolution, she had moved to Paris to report on the dramatic events unfolding there, and fallen in love with an American, Gilbert Imlay.

Smitten by his apparent embrace of her political philosophy, as well as his open American manners, she believed their relationship was based on trust, loyalty, and equality. When she became pregnant, she assumed that they would make a life together according to these egalitarian principles. But a few months after the birth of her daughter Fanny, Imlay abandoned her. Disillusioned and despairing, she realized that she was on her own. To earn a living, she would have to pretend to be married, or she and Fanny would face ostracism, and she would not be able to publish her books and articles. An unmarried mother might be acceptable in revolutionary France, but never in England, where her publisher was based.

In 1797, she and Godwin confronted the same dilemma, further complicated by the existence of Fanny. If they married, they would reveal to the world that Wollstonecraft and Imlay had not been married and that Fanny was illegitimate. On the other hand, if they did not marry, their new baby would be stigmatized. Either way, Wollstonecraft's reputation was ruined, and so was that of one child. And so, after much debate, they decided that 3-year-old Fanny would pay the price for the sake of their unborn baby—a truth that would shadow young Mary Shelley for the rest of her life.

Although they had succumbed to convention, Godwin and Wollstonecraft resisted the restraints of a typical 18th-century marriage. Wollstonecraft refused to become an ordinary wife. In a letter to Godwin, she declared, 'my time, appears to me, as valuable as that of other persons accustomed to employ themselves'. She complained if he left her in charge of dealing with the landlord, the plumbing, or 'the disagreeable business of settling with tradespeople'. In response, Godwin tried to shoulder some of the household responsibilities so that Wollstonecraft could write—an extraordinary concession for the time. In return, she agreed to contribute her earnings to the family's upkeep—another innovation in an era when middle-class men were supposed to be the sole providers for their families. Trailblazers that they were, they knew of no other couples who had made such an arrangement. One hundred and thirty years later, Virginia Woolf would look to their marriage for inspiration when she was trying to carve out her relationship with her husband Leonard. To Woolf, Wollstonecraft's marriage would become her most revolutionary act, her 'most fruitful experiment'.

The role of the father

After Wollstonecraft died, Godwin was suddenly placed in the role of being the sole parent to both Mary and Fanny, whom he had adopted earlier that year. Although he loved both girls, particularly his own daughter, Godwin, the great advocate for liberty, could be severe, even tyrannical. For all of his public celebration of the rights of the individual, he was rule-bound and adhered to the same schedule every day, no matter what needs the girls might have. He did not allow his daughters to interrupt his writing time, making it clear that his work needed to be prioritized above all else. He was proud of Mary Shelley's intelligence, allowing her to read widely in his library, introducing her to many of his famous friends, including the American exile Aaron Burr, and encouraging her to write essays and stories, but he was also her severest critic. Over the course of her writing life, she sent him her manuscripts for comments and advice. A ruthless editor, he prevented her from publishing her second novel, *Mathilda*, and did not hesitate to tell her the weaknesses of her work. He also felt free to intervene in her personal life (when she was grief-stricken, after the death of one of her children, he wrote her a severe letter, telling her to cheer up, or Percy would leave her).

Given the importance of her father in her own life, it should come as no surprise that Mary Shelley addressed the role of fathers in her written work. She paired this exploration with her advocacy for the rights of women, depicting the harm perpetrated by abusive fathers on daughters, especially when their mothers are absent, dead, or weak. She also focused on the problems caused by neglectful, foolish, or absent fathers. All of her fictional fathers were flawed, and a few were downright terrifying. Later, Mary Shelley would say that though her father loved her, he was rarely affectionate, and always distant. In one of her fictional portraits of a father and daughter based on her own relationship with Godwin, she wrote:

> [My father] never caressed me; if ever he stroked my head or drew me on his knee, I felt a mingled alarm and delight difficult to describe. Yet, strange to say, my father loved me almost to idolatry; and I knew this and repaid his affection with enthusiastic fondness, notwithstanding his reserve and my awe.

For all of his problems as a parent, Godwin did ensure that his daughter inherited the brilliant legacy of her mother. Reminders of Wollstonecraft were everywhere, from the portrait that hung in Godwin's study to the books that lined the shelves. There was even a handwritten storybook that Wollstonecraft had composed for her older daughter, Fanny.

Godwin also made sure to tell both girls stories about Wollstonecraft and he taught young Mary to read by tracing the letters on her mother's gravestone (Figure 3).

As she grew older, Mary Shelley read and reread all of her mother's books as well as her father's 'Memoir' of Wollstonecraft, a

FRONTISPIECE

In this manner, the epitaph on my mother's tomb being my primer and my spelling-book, I learned to read.——Page 9.

3. 'The epitaph on my mother's tomb being my primer and my spelling-book, I learned to read.' From *Mrs Leicester's School*, published by William Godwin.

biography of his dead wife that he wrote immediately after she died. Godwin's 'Memoir' contained many factual errors and shocked contemporary readers with its frank depiction of her sexual life, including her love affair with Imlay and Fanny's birth out of wedlock. It also repeated rumours about sexual affairs that have never been substantiated. But for Mary Shelley, the memoir was a beacon of light, a path out of the stuffy world of 19th-century London. Steeped in her mother's ideas from such an early age, her determination to emulate Wollstonecraft was foundational to her development. She hoped, like an acolyte, to carry forward her mother's spirit, finding inspiration in Wollstonecraft's belief that if society allowed women to achieve independence, the lives of all people would improve.

Chapter 2
Gothic rebellion

As a young girl, many of Mary Shelley's favourite books were Gothic tales of horror and romance. She immersed herself in the works of novelists such as Ann Radcliffe and Matthew Lewis, but also those of her parents, as they, too, had written dark and thrilling works. Gothic works were notorious for violent and shocking plots, with supernatural twists and turns, including ghosts, murders, villains, ruins, horrors, gloomy settings, secrets, innocent maidens, and evil tyrants. Frequently, the young heroines were persecuted or suffered torture of some kind. Sometimes, they persevered based on the strength of their spirit; other times, because they were rescued by a young hero. For a lonely young girl, the line between fiction and reality often blurred, and the circumstances of Mary Shelley's life helped her see herself as a Gothic heroine, persecuted and wronged by a villain, though in her case, the tyrant she faced was not an evil man, but a woman, her stepmother, Mary Jane Clairmont. As she wrote to Percy, 'I detest Mrs. G. [Mary Jane Clairmont].'

Stepmother and stepdaughter locked horns right from the beginning, although Mary Shelley was only 4 years old when they met. Their conflicts distressed everyone in the household, but fighting with her stepmother actually helped shape Mary Shelley into an independent young woman. As she grew older, with no one to advocate for her inside her own family, she learned to argue for what she wanted in the face of Mary Jane's resistance.

Mary Shelley's dislike of Mary Jane was exacerbated by the fact that before Mary Jane's arrival, she had been the star of the household. Visitors flocked to the house to meet the daughter of Wollstonecraft and Godwin. Delicate, with pale skin, coppery curls, enormous eyes, and a tiny mouth, the young celebrity did not disappoint her admirers. Visitors reported that she was the most intelligent child they had ever seen. One of her particular admirers was the poet Samuel Taylor Coleridge, who first met her in the winter of 1799 when he was 27 and Mary Shelley was 2. A devoted follower of Godwin, but even more so of Wollstonecraft, the young poet was alarmed by how well behaved the Godwin girls were. Godwin's coldness was harming the two young girls, Coleridge thought, telling his friend that they should be more like his own 3-year-old son, who rode the wind like a bird, 'using the air of the breezes as skipping ropes'. In later years, when he came to visit, he always made a point of visiting the girls and drawing them out. Fanny was shy and tended to hold back, but Mary Shelley loved hearing him tell stories and sat at his feet, entranced.

When her father married Mary Jane, Mary was immediately demoted from her position of ascendancy, as Godwin was smitten with his new wife. Even worse, Mary Jane brought two children into the marriage, Charles and Jane. Charles was about the same age as Fanny, but he was away at school much of the time and so did not figure much in the family dramas—and dramas there were. Seeing herself as a warrior for the cause of her dead mother, Mary Shelley resented everything about Mary Jane, from the special treatment she doled out to her own children to her 'usurpation' of her mother's place. Jane, who was six months younger than Mary Shelley, and admired her stepsister, took Mary Shelley's side. Fanny, insecure and shy, tried to avoid the conflicts between her half-sister and stepmother, but Jane rejoiced in the excitement, doing her best to stir up conflicts. Matters were made worse by Godwin's obvious favouritism. He ignored the other children, focusing largely on his own daughter. Jane was jealous, but, as Mary Shelley would later make clear, it was not easy to bear Godwin's scrutiny. She often felt she disappointed him, and yearned to have a mother who loved her, a dream that fuelled her hatred of Mary Jane.

And yet, despite Mary Shelley's enmity, Mary Jane was not a villain. She could be irritating, and she did favour her own children, but she was also an excellent businesswoman, keeping the family afloat financially, as Godwin was notoriously bad with money. She was also an intellectual; she had translated *The Swiss Family Robinson* from the French, and, with Godwin, started the Juvenile Library, a publishing imprint and bookstore dedicated to children's literature and educational books. Before long, she became the most prominent female publisher in London. With some help from Godwin, it is possible she and her stepdaughter could have forged a bond. But Godwin locked himself in his study and ignored their fights, allowing Mary Jane to rule the household. As for Mary Shelley, the more she fought with her stepmother, the more she longed for Wollstonecraft, imagining her as the perfect all-loving mother.

One famous conflict occurred when Mary Shelley was 8 years old. Coleridge paid the family a visit and announced that he would recite from his new poem *The Rime of the Ancient Mariner* after dinner. In the past, Godwin had always let his girls stay up late to listen to Coleridge tell stories and recite his poems, but on this particular evening Mary Jane put her foot down, and sent the children up to bed. Determined to hear her old friend's poem, Mary Shelley stole downstairs, with Jane close behind. The two girls hid behind the couch to listen to the poet, and, for the rest of Mary Shelley's life, she would be able to recall each word, reciting lines of the poem to the poets she would later come to know, ensuring Coleridge's influence on the next generation of Romantic writers, but also using many of his themes and imagery in her own work, from *Frankenstein* to *Falkner*. When Mary Jane discovered the girls, she wanted to punish them, but Godwin and Coleridge stopped her. If there had been any hope of reconciliation between stepdaughter and stepmother it was over. With this act of defiance, Mary Shelley aligned herself with her father and his friend, casting off any pretence of obedience to Mary Jane. To Mary Shelley, her stepmother stood for mediocrity and the limitations of the conventional woman's world—everything she wanted to escape, everything that her mother had fought against. Inspired by her reading of Gothic romances, it was an easy next step to make Mary Jane into a symbol, a figure of oppression—someone to set herself against, a Gothic villain.

It is to Mary Jane's credit that she always strove to take care of her angry stepdaughter, at least from a practical standpoint. She nursed her when she was sick, even accompanying her to Ramsgate as part of a cure for stubborn eczema on her arm. She took all the children on outings to the parks and theatre, and made sure their meals were healthy and their clothing suitable and clean. But for all of Mary Jane's efforts, Mary Shelley's rebelliousness only grew more pronounced. The tension escalated until, when Mary Shelley was 14, Godwin felt compelled to send her away to a family living in Dundee, Scotland. He had never actually met the Baxters, but had corresponded with them about radical politics, and apparently this was enough for him.

When Mary Shelley arrived in June 1812, Scotland was already famous as a land of romance for 19th-century literary tourists. Coleridge and the Wordsworths had made a pilgrimage there. Dorothy, the sister of the poet, declared, 'Scotland is the country above all others that I have seen in which a man of imagination may carve out his own pleasures.' Scotland was also the home of the Highlanders who had staged countless revolts against the Crown. Sir Walter Scott had published his dramatic poem 'The Lady of the Lake' in 1810 and throngs of English travellers visited the Highlands, reciting Scott's words as they hiked down gorges and gazed at plunging waterfalls. To Mary Shelley, Scott's noble heroine Ellen Douglas embodied all she hoped to become: beloved, brave, and tragic.

Although the Highlanders had surrendered by the time Mary Shelley arrived, there was still unrest in the countryside. It was illegal to play the bagpipes and the ban against wearing a tartan had only recently been lifted, as both were symbols of rebellion. Stories of brave heroes and heroines haunted the young woman's imagination. For a teenage girl, these dangers seemed thrillingly romantic. She aligned herself with the rebels, casting herself in the role of defiant freedom fighter, although her opponent was Mary Jane, not the English government.

Mary Shelley would spend almost two years in Scotland, with only one trip home. In later years, she would look back on this time as an important interlude in her development as a writer, describing Dundee as an 'eyry of freedom'. She recounted her time alone in the fields, dreaming of stories she wanted to tell. To a girl like Mary Shelley, Scotland was a magical land, wreathed in legend—the perfect place to let her imagination roam free and cultivate her sense of being a Gothic heroine. Indeed, in her second novel, *Mathilda*, the heroine spends a lonely childhood in Scotland, dreaming of the father who has abandoned her. Isabella Baxter, the youngest daughter of the household, soon became Mary Shelley's close friend and helped fuel her revolutionary spirit. Isabella revered Mary Wollstonecraft and was delighted to know her daughter. An enthusiastic student of the French Revolution, she inspired Mary Shelley by discussing the courageous feats of Charlotte Corday and Madame Roland, heroines of the Revolution, declaring that she intended to follow their example and fight tyranny in all its forms. This passionate relationship with history was a revelation for Mary Shelley. Isabella scoured the past for clues about the present, for ideas about how to live a truly revolutionary life.

Summoned home at the age of 16, Mary Shelley stepped off the ship in London, even more dedicated to the cause of rebellion than before she left. Like the Scottish Highlanders, she would be a revolutionary. Like her friend Isabella, she would emulate the radical women of the French Revolution. But back in London, her opportunities for revolution were limited. As Wollstonecraft had observed in her first book, *Thoughts on the Education of Daughters*, there were few freedoms for a young woman in Mary Shelley's position. Unless she married, she would have to remain at home with her father and stepmother. As one of the daughters of the house, it seemed unlikely that she could overthrow the rule of Mary Jane. She had no money of her own and no prospect of earning any. It also seemed unlikely that she could marry as Godwin, who had always struggled financially, was deeply in debt and few suitors would want a bride without a dowry. The only other choices for a young woman of her background were to be a teacher, a governess, or lady's companion—positions that would hardly advance the cause of freedom. For Mary Shelley, well versed in her mother's quest for independence, her life now seemed a disappointment, without liberty, without love, and with no chance to live up to the legacy of her mother. She wanted to fight her own battles of liberation. At the very least, she wanted to vanquish her opponent, Mary Jane Clairmont.

Percy Shelley

But Mary Shelley's life was about to take a dramatic turn. Before long, she would outdo even Wollstonecraft in her own bid for independence. Her father had recently met a young admirer, Percy Shelley, a radical, who was also the son of a baronet. Percy revered Godwin for his stance on political liberty and had promised to help Godwin financially in return for his advice about how to reform the world. An activist and an idealist, he had just returned from organizing protesters against English rule in Ireland.

Percy had a powerful effect on those who met him. His friend Thomas Jefferson Hogg described him as 'wild, intellectual, unearthly; like a spirit that has just descended from the sky; like a demon risen at that moment out of the ground'. Later, Mary Shelley would describe him as 'sensitive', 'impetuous', and 'generous'. He had a wicked sense of humour and a propensity for shocking people. Expelled from Oxford for writing a fiery tract announcing his atheism, his renegade behaviour recommended him to Mary Shelley. Ordinary people could not understand him, she wrote, as 'he loved to idealize reality' and dwelt 'in the wildest regions of fancy'. Godwin had told his daughter and the rest of his family that they had to win Percy's approval, as he desperately needed the young man to pay his debts. But this would turn out to be a problem, since Percy was dependent on his father for money and Sir Timothy, appalled by his son's behaviour, was currently withholding funds to ensure his son's obedience. As a result, each penny that Percy wrested from his family's estate was the result of long, bitter legal proceedings.

If Mary Shelley was eager to meet Percy, Percy was even more excited to meet the child of Godwin and Wollstonecraft, the two icons of political liberty whom he most admired. With such parents, he was sure that this young woman would be extraordinary. Months before they met, he had gazed at the large portrait of Wollstonecraft in Godwin's study intrigued to hear that young Mary was 'very much like her mother'. Two years later, he would immortalize her heritage, writing:

> They say that thou wert lovely from thy birth,
> Of glorious parents, thou aspiring Child.

When the big day came and Percy arrived at their house for dinner, it was clear to Mary Shelley that he was unlike any young man she had ever met. Right from the start, he announced his radical beliefs, as though he were trying to outdo her own father. He embraced revolution, condemned the English oppression of the Irish, thought the monarchy should be overthrown, and hated organized religion. He did not care if he shocked people. In fact, he seemed to embrace it. Even his appearance was unconventional. He wore his shirt open. His hair was long and messy. His eyes flashed when he spoke.

The two young people were drawn to each other immediately. According to Thomas Hogg, not only was Mary Shelley 'fair-haired, pale indeed, and with a piercing look', she was also wearing a tartan she had bought in Scotland to mark her support of the rebellious Highlanders and her identity as a revolutionary. Here was a woman who could match Percy's idealistic fervour.

However, there was a stumbling block: Percy was already married to an 18-year-old named Harriet Westbrook. To an ordinary young woman, this would have made Percy off limits, but Mary Shelley had read and reread the books of her parents. Wollstonecraft had condemned marriage in *A Vindication of the Rights of Woman*, and, in his first edition of *Political Justice*, Godwin had declared:

> Marriage, as now understood, is a monopoly, and the worst of monopolies. So long as two human beings are forbidden, by positive institution, to follow the dictates of their own mind, prejudice will be alive and vigorous.

Accordingly, when Percy told Mary Shelley that Harriet did not share his political philosophy, and he no longer considered himself married, Mary Shelley immediately declared her love. As Percy later recalled, she was inspired 'by a spirit that sees into the truth of things'. To her, Percy's refusal to stay with a woman he no longer loved made him seem admirable. Here was someone who listened to the dictates of his heart, not societal rules, who shared her philosophy of freedom, and wanted to live with integrity, like Wollstonecraft. However, she did not appear to think of Harriet's precarious situation. Abandoned by her husband, Harriet was left vulnerable, particularly as she and Percy already had one child, Ianthe, and were expecting a second.

Breaking the rules that were supposed to govern young ladies, she took Percy to her mother's grave where they lay on the grass in front of her mother's gravestone and, as Mary Shelley said, embraced with the 'full ardour of love'. What exactly she meant by these words is not clear, as it seems unlikely that they fully consummated their relationship in the churchyard, given all the difficulties involved: the public setting, the dangers of exposure, Mary Shelley's inexperience, and the complicated undergarments worn by 19th-century English women. Nevertheless, they marked this day as the start of their sexual relationship.

Percy immortalized this moment in the dedication of his poem *The Revolt of Islam*:

> How beautiful and calm and free thou wert
> In thy young wisdom, when the mortal chain
> Of Custom thou didst burst and rend in twain.

Mary Shelley had indeed 'burst' the 'chain of Custom'. Elated as she was, she had no idea how much she would suffer for this bold step. In Jane Austen's *Mansfield Park*, which was being readied for publication even as Mary Shelley was kissing Percy in the graveyard, pretty Maria, who runs away with a scoundrel, is cast out from society. The same would be true for Mary Shelley. She would spend much of her youth in social exile, struggling against those who blamed her for being a renegade. As the years passed, she would also have to face how much she had contributed to Harriet's heartbreak.

But at the time, this dramatic break was part of the attraction to Percy. If she wanted to be like her mother, if she wanted to be a true heroine, she needed to resist convention and embrace freedom. After all, this is what Wollstonecraft had done with

Imlay and her own father, and this is what she had defended in all of her books—liberty: the right to live one's life the way one wanted and the freedom to express one's thoughts. As a result, it did not occur to her that her father might be angry. She was sure that he, the great philosopher of freedom, the man who had recommended Percy so enthusiastically, would heartily approve.

But when Godwin and Mary Jane learned of the affair, Mary Shelley was shocked at their furious response. Mary Jane's disapproval she wrote off as yet more evidence of her mediocrity. However, her father's rage felt like a betrayal, not just of herself, but of the principles he supposedly shared with Wollstonecraft. Not only had Godwin let her down, he refused to stand up for his own ideals, and, even more importantly, those of Wollstonecraft. At no point did she seem aware of the fact that Godwin had decided to compromise his principles for her sake, and for the sake of her mother, when they had married 16 years earlier. To her, his disapproval seemed hypocritical, and served to harden her resolve to stay true to Percy. Over the years, her disappointment in Godwin never truly abated. In many of the portraits of fathers that she painted in her fiction, the fathers betray or disappoint their daughters.

Escape

On 28 July, early in the morning, the young couple fled to Paris, taking Jane with them. Why Jane came along is a mystery. Perhaps they needed her help to escape the Godwins. Maybe Percy wanted to liberate her from social convention, as this is what he felt he had done with Harriet, and now Mary Shelley. Perhaps this was the price she had extracted for serving as their secret messenger. Or, maybe he and Jane were on the cusp of an affair themselves, as all three young people had professed their commitment to free love, viewing fidelity for the sake of fidelity as hypocritical. At any rate, Mary Shelley's motivation for including her stepsister in this adventure is particularly unclear, as she and Jane still had a fraught relationship, alternating between love and jealousy.

The trio spent three difficult months wandering around Europe without enough money and when they returned to London, 17-year-old Mary Shelley was pregnant. They had hoped to be welcomed home as revolutionaries and iconoclasts. But they were shunned by everyone they had once known and were penniless, as Percy's father, scandalized by his son's behaviour, had cut off all of his funding. The three young people took inspiration from the example of Wollstonecraft, taking lodgings in Somers Town to be near Wollstonecraft's grave. Tired and sick, Mary Shelley suffered as Percy turned his attentions increasingly to Jane. Jane had already infuriated her stepsister by declaring that she, too, was an acolyte of Wollstonecraft and had decided to change her name to Claire as a symbol of her new identity. The Godwins refused to speak to Mary Shelley, though Mary Jane allowed Claire to visit the family home, and Fanny made secret visits when she could. Isolated and worried, Mary Shelley turned to books, beginning what would become a lifelong programme of self-education—a habit that she would bestow on the strongest, most resourceful heroines in her novels. Each day, she spent hours learning Greek, Latin, and Italian, and read widely, meticulously recording her reading in her diary.

Mary Shelley's commitment to her own learning was inspired in large part by her mother's emphasis on the importance of women's education. Wollstonecraft criticized those who claimed that women should only be taught those skills that would please men. Women were not the playthings of men, Wollstonecraft had declared. They were entitled to the same natural rights, and if they were allowed to have a real education not only would their own situations improve, but society would be a better place. Men would be liberated from caring for women as though they were children and would also be spared from becoming tyrants. Children, too, would benefit, as a well-educated mother would be better able to fulfil her responsibilities.

Dependent on Percy, with no money of her own, and cut off from her family, Mary Shelley was determined to become the independent woman her mother had envisioned by improving her mind and strengthening her skills as a writer. But first, she had to correct the bad habits of her youth. Although she had been allowed to read any book in Godwin's library, she had never pursued a systematic course of study. Now, she applied herself to her work, asking Shelley, the recipient of an excellent classical education, for guidance. He helped her with Greek and Latin, and together they read many of the classics of English literature, including the *Faerie Queen* and *Paradise Lost*.

Although she devoted herself to these high-minded pursuits, she still steeped herself in the Gothic novels she loved, particularly Radcliffe's *The Mysteries of Udolpho* and Lewis's *The Monk*. She also read her father's novel *St Leon* (1794), in which a French aristocrat searches for the 'elixir' to eternal life, but ends the story as a lonely wanderer. Like Victor Frankenstein and his creature, he is separated from the rest of humanity. She also reread her mother's final unfinished novel *Maria, or the Wrongs of Woman*, which begins in true Gothic fashion with a mysterious heroine locked in an asylum for reasons she does not yet know. In the preface Wollstonecraft had written that her goal was 'to portray passions' not 'manners'—a declaration that inspired Mary Shelley. She, too, wanted to capture the truth of the heart, just as Percy said she had done, when she declared her love for him in the graveyard.

In the mid-18th century, the Gothic novels that Mary Shelley loved would have been dismissed as superstitious and sensationalist, but supernatural themes had recently risen to prominence in literary circles, elevated in part by the ideas of the political philosopher Edmund Burke. In *A Philosophical Enquiry into the Origin of our Ideas of the Sublime and Beautiful*, Burke argued that terror, pain, and fear generated an experience of what he termed 'the sublime', the strongest possible feeling in the onlooker. He wrote that terror could lead one to a transcendent experience, beyond the trivialities of the mundane world. Romantic poets, in particular, embraced these principles, seeking out themes that would initiate the experience of the sublime in their readers and would assert their own poetic visions. Mary Shelley had long been exposed to the Romantic sublime through the works of her parents and their friends. Coleridge's *The Rime of the Ancient Mariner* had thrilled her with its terrifying supernatural elements: the ghost ship and the solitary figure of the Mariner, haunted by his crime of shooting the Albatross. The Mariner is cursed by the spirit 'Life-in-Death' to endure a kind of everlasting spiritual torture—he cannot die, but neither can he be fully alive. At last, he is restored to life by appreciating the beauty of the sea creatures he sees alongside the ship and emerges, transformed by his experience.

In February, Mary Shelley gave birth, prematurely, to a little girl, who died two weeks later. Night after night, she dreamed the baby lived, writing in her journal, 'Dream that my little baby came to life again—that it had only been cold and that we rubbed it by the fire and it lived.' Like the 'Life-in-Death' punishment that Coleridge's Mariner endured, these dreams revealed Mary Shelley's curse. Her mother had died *because* of her. And now her baby had died, as well, but lived on, in some sublime and terrifying way. Haunted as she was by this experience, it should come as no surprise that the idea of the dead coming back to life would be one of the central themes of *Frankenstein*, the novel that she would start writing only a year later.

That spring, she discovered that she was pregnant again, giving birth to a second child, William, in January 1816. Claire, meanwhile, had begun a love affair with the poet Lord Byron, the most famous literary figure of the period, and the most notorious. At the time, rumours were circulating that he was having an affair with his half-sister, and he was facing legal action from his estranged wife. Even his oldest friends had turned their backs on him, and he was eager to flee England. When Claire heard that he had planned a trip to Geneva that summer, she proposed joining him there with her stepsister, Percy, and baby William. Although he was lukewarm about continuing his relationship with Claire, Byron was eager to meet the daughter of Wollstonecraft and Godwin, as well as the young poet Percy, whose exploits had intrigued him from afar. As for Mary Shelley, she had long admired Byron's poetry, and she was eager to take William out of the city for the summer. The air was thick with smoke and she worried about his health. That May, they set forth for Switzerland, little realizing that they were heading toward an adventure that would shape literary history forever.

Mary Shelley

Chapter 3
Frankenstein

The year without a summer

In May 1816, after two long years of study, Mary Shelley wanted to try her hand at writing her own stories, but the literary legacy of her parents and other Gothic writers intimidated her. She wanted to follow in their footsteps, but she also wanted to be original. How could she inspire terror and awe in her reader like the writers she admired, while maintaining her integrity and her own literary vision? She was not sure she was capable of achieving this, but she wanted to try.

On the trip to Geneva, she kept notes in a journal she shared with Percy, recording the many adventures they encountered. Even though it was spring, the snow was thick and heavy, making the passes almost impossible. A volcanic eruption in Indonesia the preceding April—the world's largest explosion in over 1,500 years—disrupted weather patterns in Europe, Asia, and even North America; 1816 would become known as the year without a summer. In Switzerland, the storms raged, making the journey over the Alps a terrifying and dangerous experience—a truly 'sublime' episode for these young Romantics. They even got stuck in a blizzard, thrilling Percy, but worrying Mary Shelley and Claire, who feared they might never get free.

Later, Mary Shelley would use her account of the wintry landscape in the original edition of *Frankenstein:*

> The scenery perpetually grows more wonderful and sublime; pine forests of impenetrable thickness, and untrodden, nay, inaccessible expanse spread on every side...
>
> Never was a scene more awfully desolate. The trees in these regions are incredibly large, and stand in scattered clumps over the white wilderness; the vast expanse of snow was chequered only by these gigantic pines, and the poles that marked our road: no river or rock-encircled lawn relieved the eye...

The 'sublime' scenery, the 'awefull' desolation, the 'incredibly' large trees, the 'wilderness'—were thrillingly novelistic and she knew it. By writing down these details, she was making her first attempts to capture the sublime moment on the page, laying the foundation of *Frankenstein*, weeks before she actually began the story.

At the same time, she was also emulating the style of her mother's *Letters Written During a Short Residence in Sweden, Norway, and Denmark*, a book that her father had cherished as he thought it showed a gentler side to Wollstonecraft than *A Vindication of the Rights of Woman*. But *Letters* also revealed the complexities of Wollstonecraft's interior life and her new focus on 'passions' rather than political philosophy. While revelling in the glories of the Scandinavian summer, Wollstonecraft prioritized her emotions, thoughts, and memories. She describes wandering in the countryside, relishing the smell of the pine and the taste of fresh strawberries. Recovering from a broken heart, she finds nature at once healing and inspiring. Her solitary rambles offered an avenue toward self-revelation and the exploration of her inner world. An encounter with a waterfall induced a transcendent experience, resulting in a sublime moment for Wollstonecraft, leading her to contemplate death and her own mortality:

My soul was hurried by the falls into a new train of reflections....
my thoughts darted from earth to heaven, and I asked myself why
I was chained to life and its misery? Still the tumultuous emotions
this sublime object excited, were pleasurable; and, viewing it, my
soul rose, with renewed dignity above its cares...

Far from England, where she had long faced criticism for her
'scandalous' ideas and lifestyle, she felt liberated to take risks as a
writer. She was also released from the domestic responsibilities
that at times overwhelmed her, as a single mother with a toddler.
Mary Shelley could well understand Wollstonecraft's sense of
liberation, as she too was enjoying the distance from England.

Once they were settled in their rooms at the Hotel Angleterre on
the shores of Lake Geneva, Mary Shelley re-dedicated herself to
her reading schedule, recording in letters and her journal that she
was 'as happy as a new fledged bird'. In the evenings, they sailed
across the lake. The water was so clear that she could see all the
way to the bottom of the lake and watch the minnows drift by.
These details stayed with her and a few months later she would
use them in her description of Frankenstein's one afternoon of
happiness, on a lake with his new bride, who exclaims, 'Look at
the innumerable fish that are swimming in the clear waters, where
we can distinguish every pebble that lies at the bottom. What a
divine day! How happy and serene all nature appears.'

But Mary Shelley's pleasure was soon marred by the other English
tourists, who refused to speak to her once they learned who she
was. When she and Claire entered the public rooms, people turned
their backs or gave them hostile glares. When Byron and his
21-year-old personal physician John Polidori arrived, the social
situation became even more tense. Rumours flew about and
the press, who were always fascinated by Byron's activities, spied
on them, labelling them the 'League of Incest', declaring that

4. The Villa Diodati.

Byron was sleeping with both Mary Shelley and Claire, and that Percy probably was, too.

To escape the gossip, Percy rented a chalet called Maison Chapuis on the opposite side of the lake from the hotel. Byron and Polidori followed, moving to the beautiful Villa Diodati about fifty yards up the hillside (Figure 4). A grand stucco house with three storeys, pillars, and a capacious front porch, there was plenty of room here for Byron, Polidori, and the Shelley party to dine and enjoy long after-dinner conversations.

The genesis of *Frankenstein*

By early June, the weather grew increasingly stormy. Weeks went by without a break from the rain. The clouds hung low in the sky, blocking the view of the mountains, the Hotel Angleterre, and the villages across the lake, giving the young people a sense of being cut off from the rest of the world. At first, the group enjoyed the novelty of their isolation, but before long, they grew restless, and turned to reading ghost stories and tales of terror taken from a German collection, translated into French, under the title *Fantasmagoriana*. They also read Coleridge's poem 'Christabel', in which a serpent disguised as a woman tries to seduce an innocent maiden named Christabel. Percy was so terrified by this poem that he screamed and ran from the room. Later, he said that he had had a vision of a woman who had eyes instead of nipples on her breasts. To Byron, Mary Shelley, and the others, this fit was evidence of Percy's 'poetical' nature, as they regarded such visions as an important aspect of the creative process.

Fifteen years later, Mary Shelley would write a version of these events for her introduction to a new edition of *Frankenstein* (1831), revised for the Bentley's Standard Novel series. She left out Shelley's panicked response to 'Christabel', but told her readers a story that has since become famous. According to her account, Byron declared that they needed scarier tales than the ones from *Fantasmagoriana*. Everyone there should write a ghost story, he decided, and a winner would be selected. Truly, this was a Gothic challenge, issued in a gloomy Gothic setting, hemmed in by the fog, the mountains, and the storms—a perfect contest for these young writers.

Byron and Percy set right to work, but soon lost interest and went back to their other projects. Polidori wrote the draft of a story that would become *The Vampyre*, one of the inspirations for Bram Stoker's famous tale *Dracula*. But it was Mary Shelley who would win the challenge. The first sentence she wrote, 'It was on a dreary night of November that I beheld my man completed', seemed to unleash all that would come next, as though the story were waiting to spill onto the page. She invented a student named Victor Frankenstein, obsessed with mastering the creation of life, who cuts himself off from everyone he loves to devote himself to his ambition, using body parts stolen from graveyards and pieces from dead animals to assemble his creation (Figure 5).

Many years later, in the 1831 edition, Mary Shelley maintained that it took her a long time to come up with an idea, and that

It was on a dreary night of November
that I beheld ~~the frame on whic~~ my man completted ~~and~~
with an anxiety that almost amount
ed to agony, I collected ~~instruments of life~~
around me ~~and endeavoured~~ that I might infuse a
spark of being into the lifeless thing
that lay at my feet. It was already
one in the morning, the rain pattered
dismally against the window panes &
my candle was nearly burnt out when
by the glimmer of the half extinguish
ed light I saw the dull yellow eye of
the creature open — it breathed hard,
and a convulsive motion agitated
its limbs.

~~Oot bots~~ How can I describe my
emotion at this catastrophe, or how deli
neate the wretch whom with such
infinite pains and care I had endeavoured
to form — his limbs were in proportion
and I had selected his features & as *beautiful*
~~handsome~~ ~~handsome. Handsome;~~ Great God! his
yellow ~~skin~~ skin scarcely covered the work of
muscles and arteries beneath, his hair *of a lustrous black, &*
was flowing and his teeth of a pearly white
ness but these luxuriances only ~~formed~~
formed a more horrid contrast with
his watry eyes that seemed almost of
the same colour as the dun white
sockets in which they were set

5. Draft page of *Frankenstein* in Mary Shelley's hand.

when an idea did arrive it came in the form of a kind of waking dream, a nightmare:

> I saw—with shut eyes, but acute mental vision—I saw the pale
> student of unhallowed arts kneeling beside the thing he had put
> together. I saw the hideous phantasm of a man stretched out and
> then, on the working of some powerful engine, show signs of life,
> and stir with an uneasy, half vital motion.

These are Mary Shelley's own words, and so there seems no reason to question her story, except that both Percy and Polidori had different versions of what happened in the summer of 1816.

In the preface to the first edition, Percy makes no mention of her struggles to start her tale. Nor does he mention any dream. All he says is that the group of friends 'agreed to write such a story, founded on some supernatural occurrence'. Polidori's diary supports Percy's account. Fascinated by Mary Shelley—Byron teased him about falling in love with her—he filled his journal with details about 'Mrs. S' and did not record any delay on her part, casting doubt on her version, since if she could not come up with an idea, he would have noticed.

What seems most likely, then, is that Mary Shelley's story about how she came to write *Frankenstein* is probably just that, a story, a fiction tacked onto her larger fiction, another layer in a many-layered book. There are many reasons why the older Mary Shelley may have decided to add this preface to the 1831 edition of *Frankenstein*. In 1818, *Frankenstein* had been published anonymously and most people assumed that Percy, or even her father had written it. She had protested against this, writing to Sir Walter Scott, who had reviewed the book favourably, that she was the actual author. But, in the 1831 edition, her name would be on the cover, and she was worried about sales, as she faced financial pressures as a single mother trying to make her living as a writer. Still despised for running away with the married Percy, she knew it was dangerous to confess that she was the author of what one critic referred to as perverse and 'monstrous' fiction. If she could improve her reputation by saying that she had not consciously created the story, then it made sense to invent a tale that would deflect criticism. Talented writer that she was, she imbued her 'dream' with the kind of specific details that made it seem real:

> When I placed my head on my pillow, I did not sleep, nor could I be said to think. My imagination, unbidden, possessed and guided me, gifting the successive images that arose in my mind with a vividness far beyond the usual bounds of reverie.

Here, she presents herself as a passive recipient of 'images', implying that it is not her fault that this dream has come to her. It is 'unbidden' and 'possessed' her. Instead of asserting her claims as a creative genius, she declares that she had no agency in the story's composition—a declaration that would seem to contradict Wollstonecraft's call for women to claim their own powers.

And yet, Mary Shelley was still Wollstonecraft's daughter, as hidden behind these claims was another, prouder assertion, since, to the Romantics, a dream vision was the mark of a real writer. In the autumn of 1816, Coleridge would write a vivid description of the hallucination that led to his famous fragment of a poem, *Kubla Khan*. Percy's own vision of the woman with eyes instead of nipples had occurred just one night before Mary Shelley began writing her story.

With the story of her own dream, Mary Shelley was asserting her qualifications as a true Romantic. Sublime visions like this did not come to just anyone, at least not this kind of vivid waking dream. Only real artists could receive such momentous dreams. In other words, while she appeared to be downplaying her own role in creating the story, she was also asserting her identity as a writer. And not a simple run of the mill writer, but a chosen artist.

Sudden bursts of inspiration, vibrations from the immortals, these were the sources of art for a true poet.

But whether or not Mary Shelley actually had a dream, one thing is certain: once she began, she worked steadily, without any apparent hesitation. Percy and the others encouraged her and she hired a nurse so that she could work every day. When they returned to England that autumn, she continued writing the first draft and finished the book 18 months later.

Themes of *Frankenstein*

Drawing on her own experiences as a child whose mother had died after giving birth, who had lost her first baby, whose father had rejected her, and whose society had condemned her for living with the man she loved out of wedlock, she added an extraordinary plot twist, one that would set her story apart from others and make her one of the most famous authors in English literary history. Instead of having her young inventor feel pride in his 'completed' man, she had him reject his creation, abandoning the creature in horror.

This idea, that an inventor would be repulsed by his own handiwork, was foreign to the thinking of many Romantic poets. In *Prometheus Unbound*, the poem he started that summer, Percy celebrated creativity, imagination, and technology. According to the Greek myth, Prometheus created human beings, stole fire from Mount Olympus to give to humanity, and was punished by Zeus for eternity. In Percy's version, Prometheus resists Jupiter's tyranny and becomes a symbol of freedom, a noble, self-sacrificing hero. Essentially optimistic, Percy's vision emphasizes that Prometheus' gifts improve the lives of human beings through advances in technology and the arts. To Percy, there was nothing more sacred than the act of creation, particularly artistic creation. Artists were like gods, capable of inventing new worlds and new lives. In this sense, he was not unlike Mary Shelley's Victor

Frankenstein, dedicated to the process of creation at all costs, glorifying the act, without thinking of the consequences.

But Mary Shelley was ambivalent about the process of creation. She, too, was fascinated by the story of Prometheus, giving *Frankenstein* the subtitle 'The Modern Prometheus', but she saw the tale through a far darker lens. In her version of the myth, Mary Shelley suggested that the obsessive pursuit of creation could cause harm, particularly if pursued at the expense of human relationships. Creation for the sake of creation was not enough, and, in fact, could wreak havoc in the world. What were the responsibilities of the creator for the created? How should one care for one's creations? Children did not ask to be born. The same held true for artificial creations and inventions. It was no accident that she was haunted by Adam's words in John Milton's *Paradise Lost*, the words she used for the epigraph to *Frankenstein*:

Did I request thee, Maker, from my clay
To mould me man? Did I solicit thee
From darkness to promote me?

Her own father had cast her off, unfairly, she felt. No child deserved such harsh treatment. Every creature needed a parent; every creation deserved to be nurtured. She had suffered too much to think otherwise. Without Wollstonecraft, her upbringing had been almost unendurable. Godwin had been distant and unreachable. Children needed nurturing parents, she implied; indeed, they needed mothers, in particular. Victor Frankenstein's attempt to erase the role of women in the creation of human life wrought real damage. Without mothers, without nurturing parents, children could easily grow up to be monsters, making the world a dangerous place—cruel, and filled with hate.

Mary Shelley's empathy with the child—the artificially created being—as well as the inventor, gave her a dramatically different point of view from Percy, who was mostly interested in the act of creation and the creator himself (always male). To convey the suffering of the artificially created being, she switched her vantage point from Victor Frankenstein to that of his creature, emphasizing the *results* of Victor's actions.

The transition occurs when the creature, who has been searching for his 'father', has at last tracked Frankenstein down. At this point in the story, the creature has already committed his first murder, killing Victor's young brother and framing Justine, one of the only potentially strong female characters, as the murderer. Despite his violent acts, the creature pleads for Frankenstein's sympathy, explaining that after he awoke and found himself abandoned, his first instincts were innocent, even virtuous. He describes his high-minded attempts to educate himself, reading books, such as *Paradise Lost*, and declares, 'I ought to be thy Adam, but I am rather the fallen angel' (all quotations are from the 1818 version). Longing for companionship, he hides himself near an educated and highly refined family and tries to help them by secretly supplying them with firewood and clearing the snow from their path. He tells himself they will accept him, that they will 'overlook my personal deformity', assuring himself that when he has 'solicited their compassion and friendship' they will welcome him. But his worst fears are realized when the cottagers come face to face with him. They see his ghastly appearance and are terrified, attacking him before they flee. In revenge, the creature sets fire to their cottage (an indirect allusion to the Prometheus story), swearing eternal enmity to all of humanity and blaming his 'father' for bringing him to life.

Despite the violence the creature commits, it is difficult for the reader to condemn him, as Mary Shelley has demonstrated how he hoped to be embraced and suggests that the family's reaction is unwarranted and cruel. But the horrified Victor has no empathy for his 'son'. Instead, he rejects him yet again. Outraged and hurt, the creature says, 'If I have no ties and no affections, hatred and vice must be my portion.' He declares that he will continue his rampage of murderous revenge unless his father makes him a female companion. 'I am alone and miserable. Man will not associate with me, but one as deformed and horrible as myself would not deny herself to me. This being you must create.' Frankenstein agrees to this proposition, and sets to work on a secluded island off the coast of Scotland, until he is overcome by fear and disgust, destroying her. In response, the creature goes on a murderous rampage, killing all whom Victor holds dear, including his fiancée, Elizabeth, forcing his creator into loneliness as well.

By depicting the creature's sorrow in such vivid detail, Mary Shelley asks the reader to sympathize with him even though his 'father' cannot. The creature explains, 'I do know that for the sympathy of one living being, I would make peace with all. I have love in me the likes of which you can scarcely imagine and rage the likes of which you would not believe. If I cannot satisfy the one, I will indulge the other.' The implication is clear: if Victor were to love and nurture his creature, the creature would love him in return, and love 'all' the world. But without 'sympathy', he will become a raging child, an outlaw because of the cruel treatment of his creator.

Having emphasized that the creature yearned for 'love and sympathy' before he becomes violent, Mary Shelley underlines the point that it is Victor Frankenstein who is at fault. The creature emerges into consciousness with the 'natural' good intentions of the innocent child—an idea inspired by Jean-Jacques Rousseau. He comes to naught because of the harsh treatment he receives, not because of any inherent character flaw. Without an education, without the nurturing care of a parent, the creature becomes 'monstrous'—a point that Mary Shelley had gleaned from her mother's emphasis on the importance of education. Parents must guide and care for their children, or these neglected children will run wild and harm society. In one of his final speeches, the creature declares, 'My heart was fashioned to be susceptible to love and sympathy; and when wrenched by misery to vice and hatred, it did not endure the violence of the change without torture.'

Mary Shelley's attention to the creature's point of view adds a complicated psychological layer to her tale. Instead of elevating the creative powers of humankind—as Percy had done—she describes the destruction that ensues after Frankenstein flees from his 'completed' man. In her hands, then, *Frankenstein* is not primarily a story about creation, like Percy's triumphal tale, *Prometheus Unbound*, rather it is the story of what happens *after* the act of creation. What are the consequences of Victor Frankenstein's actions? What are his responsibilities as an inventor? What happens to the world as a result of his creation? What happens when he attempts to bypass the role of the mother? And most important of all, what happens to his neglected creation, the creature? What happens to a creature starved for love?

Robert Walton and MWS

That autumn, Mary Shelley added one more layer to the story: the perspective of Robert Walton, an Arctic explorer searching for the North Pole, who encounters Frankenstein and the creature in the wilderness. Like the Ancient Mariner, Victor feels compelled to tell his story to Walton and Walton recounts the tale in a series of letters to his sister Margaret Walton Saville, providing the reader with a third version of events.

In his account, Walton describes Victor with an admiration that borders on reverence. He is flattered when Victor says that Walton reminds him of himself, not realizing that one of the characteristics they share is selfishness. Like Victor, he pursues his ambition with destructive single-mindedness, evincing no concern for those he might hurt. Victor encourages him not to give up, even as it becomes clear that his endeavour is endangering the lives of his sailors. In his letters, Walton tries to reassure his sister, who has 'evil forebodings' about his voyage and urges him to turn back, but Walton is so obsessed with proving his own genius that he refuses to stop. He quotes from Coleridge's *Rime of the Ancient Mariner*, declaring that he will explore the land 'of mist and snow', and tells his sister he will 'kill no albatross, therefore do not be alarmed with my safety'. By alluding to this tale of catastrophe, Walton unwittingly acknowledges the dangers of his mission. The rebellion of the sailors demonstrates how deluded Walton has become, as does their refusal to continue, even after Victor gives a rousing speech, telling them that if they succeed they will 'be hailed as the benefactors of your species; your name adored, as belonging to brave men who encountered death for honor and the benefit of mankind'.

When at last he is defeated by the elements and the sailors' threat of mutiny, Walton is cast down by his failure, never realizing that his decision to turn back offers a hopeful alternative to the disastrous choices made by Victor. Even when the sailors rejoice, Walton, obsessed with his failed quest for glory, despairs, though he recognizes that if he had died in the Arctic wilderness, he would cause his sister great suffering.

Although the reader never gets to hear Margaret's point of view directly, Walton's references to her letters allow her to emerge as the voice of reason in the novel, an offstage voice, but an important one all the same. Her opposition to her brother's ambition is a crucial counterpoint to the obsessive pursuit of glory by the male characters in the novel, reminding the reader of the importance of love and relationships. That she plays a significant role in the story is hinted at when Victor's plea to Walton to kill the creature is stopped abruptly by an editorial intrusion. 'Walton, in continuation' cuts short Victor's monologue and reintroduces Walton's voice, who addresses his sister directly, writing, 'You have read this strange and terrific story, Margaret; and do you not feel your blood congealed with horror?'

Margaret never responds to this query, but Walton's question puts her squarely in the place of the novel's reader, and though there is no attribution to the editorial phrase, she would seem to be the likeliest candidate. As the recipient of Walton's letters, Margaret is the only character who could organize them and control the flow of the narrative, elevating her from an offstage voice to the mastermind behind the organization of the story. As the literary scholar Angela Wright points out, Margaret's point of view 'lies at the structural and thematic core of the tale'. For the reader, it is easy to miss her importance, as we never hear her voice directly, but her vantage point is crucial to the tale, as at no point does she endorse her brother's quest, or express any admiration for his heroics. Instead, her criticism remains under the surface of the tale, unspoken, but powerfully present in her brother's invocations.

Margaret's significance, and the closeness Mary Shelley felt to her, is underscored by the fact that she gave Margaret the initials she would have if she were married to Shelley and if Godwin was erased from her name: MWS. Mary Wollstonecraft Shelley. Though Margaret's point of view is filtered through her brother's letters, her critique of her brother disrupts his attempts to present himself or Victor as a hero. By embedding Margaret in the story, Mary Shelley prevents the male characters from achieving the apotheosis they seek. Her critical viewpoint serves as an invaluable counterpoint to the self-serving accounts of the men.

By providing the reader with Margaret's point of view, as well as three different versions of the same set of events, Mary Shelley wrote a complicated story that is far more than a simple parable against the dangers of invention, a reading of the text that persists today. Instead, the central themes of the story, derived as they are from Wollstonecraft, include the importance of education and human connection, as well as the importance of mothers and mothering, but there are other important ideas as well. Mary Shelley points to the dangers of the male pursuit of glory when achieved at the expense of others, particularly women. She also includes Romantic ideas about the imagination, reading, writing, and the sublime. In the preface to the second version, she suggests that the novel is also about the origins of life, recounting conversations between Percy and Byron, where the two men discussed experiments that used electricity to animate inanimate objects and wondered if a corpse could be 'reanimated' by these 'extraordinary measures'—an idea with obvious resonances for Mary Shelley, haunted as she had been by the death of her mother and her first child. In her version of events, she does not contribute to the conversation between the two men. Instead, she presents herself as a listener, like Margaret—a woman who hears and distils the conversations of men, but does not speak herself, except offstage, or, in this case, later, and on paper.

Accordingly, although it is clear that the creation of life is an essential component of the story, Mary Shelley does not allow the book to be about a single theme. By including the different points of view, she shifts the focus of the book to the complexities of the human heart and human relationships. Ultimately, she raises many questions: what does it mean to be a human being? Who in the story is most human? The creature? Frankenstein? Walton? Margaret? What happens when Frankenstein attempts to erase the role of the mother? The creature's poignant story and his yearning for human connection allows Mary Shelley to suggest that if Frankenstein had relented and had 'sympathy' for the creature, he could have become a positive member of society, despite his 'fearsome' appearance. Sympathy, then, and love would seem to be one of the most important components of a human being—components that Frankenstein and Walton lack, but which the creature has, at least before he is corrupted by society. And which Margaret seems to possess as well.

Frankenstein and Wollstonecraft

Mary Shelley dedicated the novel to her father, writing that the book was 'respectfully inscribed' to William Godwin. The restraint of this dedication reflected the fact that she and her father were still not speaking. Indeed, despite this dedication, *Frankenstein* can be read as an expression of longing for her own mother as well as an impassioned evocation of the importance of mothers, in general. By articulating the pain of the motherless creature and describing the damage done by Frankenstein's abandonment of his responsibilities, she was able to demonstrate the tragedy that ensues when parents do not love and guide their children, a theme that she would continue to develop in subsequent works, emphasizing the importance of a healthy, nurturing relationship between parents and children. Her concern about the abandonment of children also stemmed from a belief that she shared with other Romantics, that children were innocents who needed to be protected. According to this philosophy, children were closer to Nature than adults, and should therefore serve as guides to society; it was the world that was corrupt, not children. The next step seemed inevitable: if all human beings came into the world as innocent creatures, then violent, unstable adults were the result of neglect, bad education, and a diseased society.

Despite these Wollstonecraftian themes, at first reading, *Frankenstein* seems to owe nothing to the principles of *A Vindication of the Rights of Woman*, as there are no strong female characters, no pronouncements advocating for women's rights, and no statements about the importance of women's education or independence. By the end of the novel, all of the female characters are dead, except for Safie, one of the cottage inhabitants whom the creature attempts to befriend, and Margaret Walton Saville, who, despite her importance, remains resolutely offstage. Ultimately, the world Mary Shelley paints is one in which women are unable to exert any power and raw male ambition lays waste to society and to intimate relationships. And yet, by demonstrating the violence that occurs when women are not allowed to play an active part in shaping the world, Mary Shelley makes a strong case for the significance of women's roles. If women are ignored, destroyed, or dismissed, she implies, then unchecked male passion will destroy civilization. Relationships will be torn apart. Without strong women, the world will be devoid of meaning, love, and balance, destroyed by men, who are ruled by their passion for fame, invention, and achievement. The silent, critical voice of Margaret comes to bear, enacting judgement against the excesses of Walton, Frankenstein, and the creature. Importantly, it is this voice that will emerge more clearly in Mary Shelley's later work.

Tragedy

While Mary Shelley was writing *Frankenstein*, two events occurred that served to underscore the dystopian themes of the book. Her half-sister Fanny and Harriet Shelley, Percy's first wife, both killed themselves, highlighting the grim truth that Mary Shelley already knew: unmarried mothers and illegitimate children were hated by society and driven to despair, just like Frankenstein's creature. Her own mother had become an outcast when she gave birth to Fanny out of wedlock and had tried to commit suicide twice. Fortunately, she had been rescued but her plight as an unmarried mother isolated her, causing her enormous psychological pain. Fanny, too, had been rendered an outcast by society's strictures. To Mary Shelley, the suffering of her mother and half-sister was unpardonable: Wollstonecraft was innocent, as all she had done was fall in love, which was certainly not a criminal act, and Fanny was just a child, born through no fault of her own. Certainly, she had not asked to be brought to life, any more than Frankenstein's creature had.

As for Harriet, her death was an even more complicated burden to bear. For the rest of her life, Mary Shelley blamed herself for participating in Harriet's tragedy by running away with Shelley. Now Harriet had joined the pantheon of women who had been rendered monstrous by society, cast away by the world. Even worse, Mary Shelley benefited from Harriet's death. With Harriet gone, she and Percy were now free to wed; they married in December 1816. For Mary Shelley, who marked the wrong date down on her calendar, her wedding only served to underscore the injustices of English marital law. It had taken Harriet's death to free Percy, as divorce, for any reason, was almost impossible.

In response to these suicides, Mary Shelley experienced a complicated mix of emotions, including regret, sorrow, rage, and guilt—all of which she poured into her novel. She felt a kinship with Fanny and her mother, and, now, Harriet. She had been punished by her father, and by society for loving Percy. She worried that Claire, who was pregnant with Byron's child, would soon join this club of outcast women and that her child would join the ranks of rejected children. Although she could not retaliate against society's cruelty by going on a murderous rampage, she could imagine such a rampage and describe it in vivid, visceral detail. The creature would take revenge on her behalf. But it was also true that she saw herself as complicit in the deaths of all three women. Her birth had resulted in her mother's death. The expectation of her arrival had prompted Godwin and Wollstonecraft's marriage, exposing Fanny's illegitimacy. And Harriet had killed herself because she, Mary Shelley, had run away with Harriet's husband.

Mary Shelley spent the spring of 1817 readying the manuscript of *Frankenstein* for publication, finishing before she gave birth to her third child in September. The significance of the book's gestation period was not lost on her. As the scholar Anne Mellor points out, she referred to the book as her 'offspring', linking the story to her own birth. The tale begins on Dec 11 17— and ends in Sept 17—. Mary Wollstonecraft conceived in early December 1796, gave birth to Mary on 30 August 1797, and died on 10 September 1797. These connections to her own birth suggest Mary Shelley's closeness to her story. Like Frankenstein, she was driven by the ambition to create, in her writing and as a mother. Like the creature, she felt abandoned by her creator, as her birth had been followed by the death of her mother, resulting in a fatal quandary. Wollstonecraft could only have survived if she had not been conceived. And if she had not been conceived, she could never have brought *Frankenstein* to life. By framing the novel with Walton's letters to 'MWS', another self-reflection, it is as though she wrote the tale for herself, becoming both author and audience, author and editor, creator and created, mother and daughter, inventor and destroyer, Frankenstein and his creature, and, of course, Mary Wollstonecraft Shelley (author) and MWS (character and editor)—the female voices of reason who control the story, but are sidelined from the action.

In her subsequent work, Mary Shelley would allow this silent voice to speak. Where the men in *Frankenstein* dominate the narrative, retelling horrors with no restraint, it is the woman's point of view that she would focus on in her later work. Increasingly, she would shine a light on the strength of reasonable women, allowing them to occupy more important roles, until, at the end of her career, it would be the female characters who would triumph over the weakness of the men, leading the way to a new world where horror was restrained by good judgement, where reason reigned over violence. For Mary Shelley, rewriting the balance of the world was as important a mission as writing *A Vindication of the Rights of Woman* had been for her mother. Deeply moved by the deaths of Fanny and Harriet, she knew that if she wanted to make the world a less dangerous place for women, particularly women who lived outside the pale, she needed to give them the spotlight, and allow their suffering and their triumphs to occupy centre stage. Only then, would audiences learn to have sympathy for them and, even more importantly, come to respect, and maybe even embrace, their points of view.

Chapter 4

Early female narrators: *A History of a Six Weeks Tour Through a Part of France, Switzerland, and Holland* and *Mathilda* (1817–1821)

Anonymity

There was no trumpet call, no flurry of announcements in the press when Mary Shelley made her literary debut. Having returned to England in the autumn of 1816, she and Percy continued to be reviled by the English press and excluded from London society despite the fact that they were now married. Claire, who gave birth to Byron's baby in the spring of 1817, lived with them, and many believed that Percy was the father of her little girl, Allegra. The Godwins accepted Mary Shelley's relationship with Percy now that they were wed, but most people still regarded them with suspicion, as dangerous radicals and rule-breakers.

In the midst of such a hostile environment, it made sense for Mary Shelley to avoid yet more criticism by starting her career anonymously, but this meant her entrance into the literary world was silent as the tomb. She published two books within three months of each other, *A History of a Six Weeks Tour Through a Part of France, Switzerland, and Holland* in November 1817 and *Frankenstein* in January 1818. Although the secrecy protected her from slander, particularly from those who criticized her for running away with Percy, the result was that, like her fictional counterpart, Margaret Walton Saville, Mary Shelley's role as editor and author was almost invisible to the public. The fate of her third book, *Mathilda*, which she wrote two years after *Frankenstein*, was even more dispiriting. She wrote it while abroad in Italy, and sent it to her father for his editorial advice, but he stopped its publication entirely, deeming it too scandalous for public consumption.

Six Weeks (1817)

Although Mary Shelley's first published work, *A History of a Six Weeks Tour Through a Part of France, Switzerland, and Holland* (*Six Weeks*) is less well known than *Frankenstein*, it is a fascinating counterpoint to the famous novel. Ostensibly a joint creation with Percy, in actuality, Mary Shelley wrote most of the material and oversaw the book's organization; Percy contributed the 'preface', the poem 'Mont Blanc', and a few observations in the first and second sections, based on letters and the shared journal that they kept during their trip to Europe in 1814, but she was responsible for everything else, including the second section of four 'letters' from 1816, two of which she had written to Fanny when they lived in Geneva; the third and fourth were a compilation of her journal entries and one of Percy's letters. She placed 'Mont Blanc' at the end of the book, representing the book's creative apex.

In *Six Weeks*, instead of being an offstage presence, like Margaret Walton Saville, she positions herself as an active commentator, editor, and speaker, filling the pages with her first-person reflections, opinions, and insights. Towns are 'disgusting' or 'divine'. On their first trip to Europe in 1814, she and her unnamed companions (Percy and Claire) make what she calls the 'eccentric' decision to walk across France for the sheer 'romance' of it. They buy an ass for her to ride, 'as I was too weak' to walk as far as the others, but Percy sprains his ankle and has to ride the donkey, leaving the two women to struggle along behind, laden with their cases and supplies. She records their meals—'stinking bacon, sour bread'—and where they slept—in barns, on straw, or upright in chairs to avoid the fleas—along with careful descriptions of the countryside. But she wanted *Six Weeks* to be more than a travelogue. Modelling the book on Wollstonecraft's *Letters from Sweden*, she includes her ideas about art, local customs, and geography, as well as her own thoughts and emotions. She has 'feelings of exquisite delight' on the shores of Lake Lucerne, but is repulsed by the other travellers on their barge trip down the Rhine. She also expresses her radical political views with ringing clarity:

> All those of every nation in Europe who have a fellow feeling with the oppressed…cherish an unconquerable hope that the cause of liberty must at length prevail.

As the scholar Paul Stock observes, Mary's use of the word 'liberty' signals to her readers that she is committed to political reform. True lovers of freedom, she declares, will unite and overturn the 'detested dynasties' of monarchical governments. She also summons the ideal of 'the sentimental community', a term that the critic Margaret Cohen argues was first used by 18th-century writers Jean-Jacques Rousseau, Germaine de Staël, and others. This idea, which she would develop in her later fiction, was based on the principle of sympathy for the 'oppressed', and an emotional connection amongst reformers that would transcend differences of nationality, class, race, and gender, leading to the successful resistance to tyranny. She articulates her stance against war, calling it a 'plague', and describes France after the Napoleonic wars as a country 'pillaged and wasted'. She makes a special point of recording 'the distress of the inhabitants, whose houses had been burned, their cattle killed, and all their wealth destroyed'—observations that she would later develop in her historical novels *Valperga* and *The Fortunes of Perkin Warbeck*.

While Mary Shelley was recording her political observations, leaders from Britain and Europe were meeting in the Congress of Vienna in an attempt to prevent the rise of another leader like Napoleon. Although Mary Shelley, like other liberals, was inspired by and supported the international attempt to preserve peace, she joined with others in hoping the Congress would push forward reforms based on human rights. But she was to be disappointed. Although the Congress re-established the boundaries of European states and forged new treaties, creating a 40-year peace that did not end until the First World War, the reforms that she and others hoped for never came to pass. Indeed, the monarchical system was preserved throughout Europe and 'the oppression' of working people continued unabated, infuriating reformers, such as Percy and Mary Shelley.

On their return to Europe in 1816, she focuses less on politics and more on the sublimity of the landscape, describing the enormous impact of witnessing Mont Blanc for the first time:

> I never knew—I never imagined what mountains were before. The immensity of these serial summits excited, when they suddenly burst upon the sight, a sentiment of ecstatic wonder, not unallied to madness.

Influenced as she was by the Romantic sublime in Coleridge and the writing of her own parents, she views the landscape as important for the psychological impact it has on the onlooker. In this case, her encounter with Mont Blanc becomes a transcendent moment, lifting her out of the mundane world into the world of wonder. Although these passages are the basis for her descriptions of the landscapes in *Frankenstein*, there is little else to suggest that the same author has written both books. Indeed, the style and themes of the two volumes seem so different that the contemporary reading public can be forgiven for not recognizing the same hand in both.

For Mary Shelley, though, the two books were closely linked. Based on letters and journal entries from their time in Geneva, the second section of *Six Weeks* was written at the same time that she began

Frankenstein. In fact, the idea for the book had been percolating the whole time she was working on her famous novel. Accordingly, it did not take her long to ready the manuscript of *Six Weeks* for publication. After she finished *Frankenstein*, she began to edit the letters and diary entries that would form the basis of *Six Weeks*. Having decided not to write new material, she confined herself to condensing and extending the writing she had done while abroad. She and Percy were living in the English countryside during this period, and although she was in the final trimester of her third pregnancy and had just finished more than a year of sustained effort on *Frankenstein*, she worked on the new book with energy and characteristic self-discipline, putting the last touches to the manuscript after she gave birth to Clara on 2 September 1817.

In *Six Weeks*, Mary Shelley explores all that she had left out of her novel, describing what it was like to be a young Englishwoman in Europe, with Romantic sensibilities, liberal politics, and an active curiosity. Indeed, *Six Weeks* can be read as the inverse of *Frankenstein*, revealing the world as seen through the eyes of a young woman, the very perspective that is lacking in the novel. The letters she includes are the letters she wrote to Fanny, giving them an added poignancy, as they serve as a kind of memorial to her dead half-sister. She records the halcyon days in Switzerland with Percy, exactly the sorts of days that Victor never gets to enjoy with his bride, Elizabeth:

> our time passes swiftly and delightfully. We read Latin and Italian during the heats of noon, and when the sun declines we walk in the garden of the hotel, looking at the rabbits, relieving fallen cockchafers, and watching the motions of a myriad of lizards, who inhabit a southern wall of the garden.... in my present temper of mind, the budding flowers, the fresh grass of spring, and the happy creatures about me that live and enjoy these pleasures, are quite enough to afford me exquisite delight, even though clouds should shut out Mont Blanc from my sight.

What she does not say was that these were the pleasures that Fanny had never had the opportunity to experience. The world had been a hostile place for a young woman like her half-sister, born out of wedlock, unwanted, and a perpetual reminder of her parents' illicit relationship.

Six Weeks was positively reviewed but did not sell well. The young couple, who were perennially short of money, turned their hopes to *Frankenstein*, but in one of the great ironies of literary history, *Frankenstein* would earn few royalties for its author. When *Frankenstein* was published, reviewers called it 'horrible and disgusting'. The *Monthly Review* disparaged it as 'uncouth' and utterly amoral. And yet, the novel's shocking story did catch people's attention and there was much speculation about the identity of the author. Most people assumed it was Percy, not only because of the scandalous narrative and the violent scenes but because he had written the preface to the book and the dedication was to his father-in-law. No one suspected Mary Shelley, as it seemed impossible that a woman could write such a 'monstrous' tale.

Leaving England

After the financial failure of *Frankenstein*, Mary Shelley and Percy turned their hopes for income to the long poem, *The Revolt of Islam*, which Percy had written that summer. But *Islam* had even fewer sales than *Frankenstein*. Critics largely ignored the poem and the few grudging reviews that did appear attacked Percy personally, calling him an atheist, scolding him for his 'vile' political views, and blaming him for Harriet's suicide.

Discouraged by the hostile reception of their work, the couple began to make plans to leave England. They had not been abroad since their summer in Geneva and they missed the experience of living far from England, in a community with other like-minded artists. In 1817, Percy had gone to court to try to win custody of the two children he had with Harriet, but had been dealt a severe blow, as the court took the unusual step of ruling against him, assigning the guardianship of 3-year-old Ianthe and 2-year-old Charles to Harriet's parents. In the 19th century, a father's rights were rarely questioned in such cases, but perceptions about Percy's 'immorality' had cost him dearly. Mary Shelley worried that the negative articles in the paper could provoke more legal proceedings, as the prosecution had also threatened to take William and Clara away during Percy's battle for custody. Even worse, she was concerned that if people found out who really wrote *Frankenstein* they might declare her an unfit mother.

In the spring of 1818, almost two years after their sojourn in Switzerland, and just a few months after the publication of *Frankenstein*, they decided to follow the lead of Byron, who had gone to live in Italy. They packed up their belongings and set forth in March, taking Claire and Allegra with them. Mary Shelley was filled with excitement. Percy was suffering from a variety of physical ailments and she always worried about the health of her children. Surely, the sunny climate of Italy would improve her family's well-being. She also liked the idea of leaving behind all of the prejudices of English society. It was these judgements and restrictive social mores that had brought Fanny and Harriet to take their own lives, she believed. Italy offered her the opportunity to live more freely and to gain distance from the ghosts of both young women, who still haunted her dreams.

Italy

When they arrived in Italy on 30 March 1818, Mary Shelley's joy spilled over into her journals and letters. Everywhere she looked, she saw beauty. On 6 April she wrote, 'the fruit trees all in blossom and the fields green with growing corn'. She and Percy had read Homer to prepare for their trip and were eager to see the land of classical antiquity. 'In Italy', she exclaimed, 'we breathe different air and everything is pleasant.' The children's health improved, just as she had hoped. And Percy, too, felt stronger.

One of their goals was to introduce Byron to his child, assuming that if Byron wanted custody of Allegra he would allow Claire to remain in contact with her 15-month-old. But they had not reckoned with Byron's autocratic nature. He did not want to see Claire, he declared, and wrote demanding that Allegra be sent to him in Venice. Claire was broken-hearted at the prospect of parting with her toddler, but there was nothing she could do. Byron was the father, and as such had all the power.

All three wept when they bade farewell to the little girl. Mary Shelley tried to reassure Claire that Allegra would have a far more successful future if Byron acknowledged her as his daughter than if she remained the sole daughter of an unwed mother, with no money, no reputation, and no family. No one wanted her to share Fanny's fate. But it was with heavy hearts that they travelled south-west to Livorno and settled in the three-storey Villa Bertini, perched high in Bagni di Lucca, a fashionable resort, a day's ride from Livorno. It was an easy walk to town, and yet it was also private, as the house was surrounded by a tall, thick hedge. On 15 June, Mary wrote to her friend Maria Gisborne, exulting in their good fortune. 'When I came here,' she declared, 'I felt the silence as a return to something very delightful from which I had long been absent.' Soon, they settled into a routine, reading, writing, and exploring the countryside. They had brought a nursemaid from England who helped Mary look after 2-year-old William, whom they called Wilmouse, a busy toddler, intent on exploring the world around him. Ten-month-old Clara napped and smiled at her mother and aunt. Mary Shelley had never been happier.

But tragedy was soon to strike. Late that summer, Byron agreed to let Claire visit her daughter. She left Bagni di Lucca in high spirits, but once she arrived in Venice, she wrote a frantic letter, demanding Percy come to help her deal with Byron's drunkenness and unstable moods. She was worried for Allegra's safety. Percy set forth at once, leaving Mary Shelley with the two children. She did not like Percy and Claire to spend too much time alone, but she did not think it wise to travel in the heat of the summer with two small children. Then, after Percy left, Clara developed a fever. She wrote to Percy that she feared for Clara's health, but Percy wrote back, reassuring her about Clara and asking her to come to Venice. To Mary Shelley, this response seemed heartless, and appallingly selfish. Did he not care about the health of their little girl? The weather was oppressive, the journey long. Still, Claire's intimacy with Percy troubled her, and so, when Percy wrote again, begging her this time, she made the decision to go. For three days, she held the feverish Clara on her lap, willing the little girl to survive the long bumpy trip. But despite her efforts, Clara's health steadily worsened. When at last they arrived, the toddler rallied for a short while, but her fever rose sharply and, a few weeks later, she died in Mary Shelley's arms. To Percy's horror, she refused to let go of the child's body and he had to tear the little girl from her arms. He buried Clara on the Lido, while Mary Shelley mourned in her room, recording her child's death in the same notebook where she had marked the deaths of Fanny and Harriet, writing, 'This is the Journal book of misfortunes.' Having lost another child, she feared that she herself was the problem. She had been the cause of her mother's death. She had lost her first daughter and now Clara. In her despair, Fanny's death, and Harriet's, too, seemed to be her fault.

Unable to forgive herself, she retreated into a stony, impervious silence, certain that she was being punished for the harm she had caused others. Maybe this was Harriet's revenge. Percy mourned her absence, but she refused to smile at him, blaming him as much as she blamed herself. If he had not begged her to come to Venice, Clara would still be alive.

They had planned to go to Naples that winter, and Percy decided they should still go, as the landscape was lovely and the weather mild, but Mary Shelley remained lost in grief. In January, Wilmouse celebrated his third birthday. The little boy was lively and strong, but she still worried about his health. Not until the end of February, when they set forth for Rome with Claire, did she feel a lifting of her spirits.

Delighted to be in the ancient city, she drew closer to Percy, exploring the nooks and crannies together. They went for long rambling walks, with 3-year-old Wilmouse trotting along next to them, holding their hands, exclaiming 'O Di che bella' at the marvels his parents pointed out. Mary Shelley was proud of William's fluency in Italian and enjoyed seeing Rome through the eyes of a child. On 12 March, she described him for her friend Marianne Hunt, 'Our little Will is delighted with the goats and the horses and the ladies white marble feet', giving us a glimpse of her 3-year-old, tall enough to enjoy the naked toes of the statues his parents admired. For both Percy and Mary Shelley, Wilmouse was even more precious after the death of Clara. Fortunately, his health was good, though both parents fussed over him, instituting a regime of cold baths to keep him strong.

In April, Mary Shelley realized she was pregnant again. Filled with hope, she and Percy spent their mornings writing in the open air. Their life in this old city seemed charmed, almost as perfect as she had dreamed it might be. But in May, all of her pleasure vanished. Wilmouse fell ill, complaining of a stomach ache. The doctor diagnosed worms, but the little boy did not recover. Over the course of a week, he grew steadily sicker as she watched helplessly. In the first week of June, she recognized that he was going through the 'convulsions of death' that Clara had endured nine months earlier. On 5 June, she wrote to her friend Maria Gisborne, 'The hopes of my life are bound up in him', and, at noon on 7 June, William died; Mary Shelley's third child was gone (Figure 6). Malaria, or Roman fever, was the final diagnosis. Percy wept, but Mary Shelley was inconsolable. On 29 June, she wrote to Marianne Hunt, 'I ought to have died on the 7th of June.'

With Claire, they moved to the countryside north of Livorno. Wrung out with grief and exhausted from her pregnancy, Mary

6. **William Shelley, aged 3 (1819) by Amelia Curran.**

Shelley stopped writing in her journal. She could hardly bear to talk to Percy or Claire. If she were not pregnant, she might have considered suicide, writing to Marianne Hunt that she was 'not fit to live'. Tortured by the sameness and the silence of the days, she finally picked up her pen in August, starting the new novel that her father would declare too shocking to be published in her lifetime. Fuelled by desolation, she wrote quickly, finishing the story in six weeks.

Mathilda (1819)

She named the book after her heroine Mathilda. Like *Frankenstein*, this eponymous novel explores the consequences of male obsession and power. But this time, Mary Shelley places a female character centre stage, allowing her fictional heroine to shape the narrative as she herself had shaped the story in *Six Weeks*. Even more importantly, Mathilda is the *only* narrator. Mary Shelley does not allow anyone else to contest Mathilda's version of events—a departure from *Six Weeks*, where she gave Percy room to provide his point of view on their journey, and from *Frankenstein*, with its layered narrative structure.

Originally, she had conceived of the story as a continuation of one of her mother's unfinished works, 'The Cave of Fancy'—a tale that resonated for the grief-stricken Mary Shelley, as it painted a desolate world, filled with mourning and disappointment. But as she worked on her story, it soon grew darker than even her mother could have imagined. In Mary Shelley's tale, Mathilda writes her life story for her friend, the poet Woodville, as she lies on her deathbed, having made the decision to kill herself, through self-inflicted consumption.

There are many parallels between Mathilda and her author. Mathilda, like Mary Shelley, is a writer. Like Mary Shelley, she lost her mother in childbirth. But these similarities do not mean that Mary Shelley intended the novella to be read as autobiographical. As Jenny DiPlacidi notes, Mary Shelley resisted such reductive readings of her fiction. For Mary Shelley, the importance of her work lay in its embodiment of her ideas, particularly her stance against male tyranny, and not as a record of her personal experiences.

Right from the beginning, Mathilda's story diverges from Mary Shelley's. For the first sixteen years of her life, Mathilda's father is absent. When he returns, she is at first delighted by their closeness, but when he grows increasingly gloomy, she worries about his dark moods and pushes him to reveal the source of his unhappiness. At length, he confesses that he harbours an incestuous love for her, and rushes away. Mathilda gives chase, like the creature chasing after his father in *Frankenstein*, but when at length she finds him, she discovers that he has killed himself. Filled with regret for pushing him to confess his feelings, she retreats from the world and determines that her life is no longer worth living. On her deathbed, she utters the words that Wollstonecraft told Godwin her own mother had spoken on her deathbed, 'A little patience, and all will be over', a speech that Wollstonecraft had also given the dying mother of her heroine in her last novel, *Maria*.

Mary Shelley italicized these words to underscore the novella's connection to Wollstonecraft. As Wollstonecraft had argued in *The Rights of Woman*, women had no legal or political recourse when victimized by men. Mary Shelley dramatizes her mother's point by demonstrating the havoc that Mathilda's father wreaks in his daughter's life. Unchecked male power is not only unjust, she suggests, it is dangerous for all involved.

When Mathilda suffers at the hands of her father, she does not react with rage. Nor does she seek revenge, like the creature in *Frankenstein*. Instead, she asserts her agency by criticizing her father's excesses and choosing to be *unlike* him. We never get to hear his version, since, unlike *Frankenstein*, there is no battle between the narrators. As the sole storyteller, Mathilda controls the course of events. She confesses that in childhood, she dreamed of union with her absent father, but, unlike her father, who is unable to control his feelings when he meets her again as a teenager, she is now horrified by these desires. By relegating them to the past, she demonstrates more maturity and self-control than her father, triumphing over his disturbing fantasies by asserting her truth, telling a survivor's tale.

Although she decides to commit suicide like her father, Mathilda's death is a slow, considered act, one of agency, not passion. As Michelle Faubert argues, Mary Shelley depicts Mathilda's choice as 'virtuous, honourable, and even socially beneficial'. Like other Romantic authors, Mary Shelley used the theme of the noble suicide to explore questions of free will and individual agency, but in Mary Shelley's case, she also presented Mathilda's suicide as a powerful critique of the patriarchal system in which she lived. By the end of her life (and the end of her story) Mathilda's pain ebbs as a result of her decision to die. She no longer feels 'horror' when she contemplates her father's suicide and declares that she has stopped brooding over his corpse, saying, 'I will not continue to trace this frightful picture.' As Angela Wright points out, rather than focusing on horror and passion, like Victor and Walton, Mathilda turns the reader's attention to renewal and beauty, ending the novel with an image of regeneration: 'the turf will soon be green on my grave, and the violets will bloom on it'. Mathilda's voice is not yet the voice of reason of Mary Shelley's future heroines; but it is the voice of female agency that, absent from *Frankenstein,* characterizes Six *Weeks.* Unlike Walton and Frankenstein, who emphasize the terrifying details of their tales and are clearly imprisoned by their passions, Wright argues that Mathilda refuses to fall into the abyss of her father's dark story, separating herself from his 'corrupted' narrative.

Mary Shelley may have intended Mathilda's suicide to be a sign of her strength and independence, but this does not make the novella's conclusion a happy one. Deeply wounded by her father, Mathilda cannot go on to live a full life. That she must die to achieve freedom from her pain is a bitter condemnation of the society in which she lives; her father's lust has effectively caused her to erase herself, a response that may be noble, and even brave, but is still a tragedy. For, as Mary Shelley makes clear, what kind of choice is this: suffering or death? What kind of world leads a virtuous young woman to choose non-being instead of life?

Mary Shelley reinforces the tragedy of her tale by emphasizing her heroine's talents and virtue, indicating that Mathilda could have lived a life of great value, if she had not been harmed by her father. She underlines Mathilda's Romantic delight in the natural world, giving Mathilda a passionate connection to nature and a purity achieved through suffering intense emotion: 'My greatest pleasure was the enjoyment of a serene sky amidst these verdant woods: yet I love all the changes of Nature; and rain, and storm, and the beautiful clouds of heaven brought their delights with them.' At the same time, she makes it clear that Mathilda would never have wanted to die if it were not for her father. 'If pain can purify the heart,' Mathilda says, 'mine will be pure.'

Although Mary Shelley does not excuse Mathilda's father, she does suggest that Mathilda's father is himself a victim of the patriarchal system. If he had not been allowed to satisfy his every whim and had received a better education, he might have been better able to exercise his talents and lead a virtuous life. But as a wealthy white man, he has never experienced any checks on his desires or his power. Early on, he fed his imagination with 'sickly' romances, learning to indulge his impulses, not restrain them. Even more troubling, as Deanna Koretsky points out, incest often suggests a disastrous wish for racial and ethnic homogeneity. By uniting with Mathilda, he can keep the outside world at bay, preserving his own power and the purity of his own blood line.

In contrast, Mary Shelley presents Mathilda's mother Diana as an ideal figure. Having been taught by her father—one of the few good fathers in Mary Shelley's fiction—to value education over impulse, and reason over emotion, Diana lives a life of self-discipline and virtue. As a wife, she serves as a moderating influence, restraining her husband's volatility. But after her death, her husband cannot control his emotions, destroying himself and his daughter with his excesses. By painting this idealistic portrait of Diana, Mary Shelley emphasizes Mathilda's loss when her mother dies. If Diana had lived, she would have been able to contain her husband and protect her daughter. In addition, she would have given Mathilda an excellent education. But instead, Mathilda is immediately vulnerable when Diana dies, making Mary Shelley's point clear: without strong mothers and wives, the world is a dangerous place for daughters. To Mary Shelley, uncontrolled patriarchal power was clearly dangerous for everyone, including the patriarchs themselves. Women needed to be empowered to offer an alternative mode of being, one based on love, education, and cooperation rather than on aggression and ambition.

When Mary Shelley sent the manuscript to her father, he was appalled and refused to send it to a publisher. Although some scholars have suggested that Godwin thought the novella was too autobiographical, what seems more likely is that he was trying to keep the family away from further scandal as the reputations of Mary Shelley, Percy, Byron, and Claire had already been tainted by rumours of incest during their sojourn in Geneva. Mary Shelley did not argue with her father, as she did not want another rupture with him, but this was a significant loss for her career, as the novel was short, easy to read, and could well have been popular, suited as it was to the era's taste for melodrama.

But there is another reason that Godwin might have loathed *Mathilda*. Mary Shelley's indictment of a bad father, and of a world without mothers, in which women are prevented from occupying leadership roles, either inside the family or out, was also an implicit condemnation of Godwin himself. This was not a new theme: in *Frankenstein*, Victor is a terrible father, abandoning his creature. With neither father nor mother, the creature turns to violence. But in *Mathilda*, Mary Shelley makes this point even more clearly. Mathilda's father is the villain of the story, particularly in contrast to Diana's ideal father. The motherless Mathilda seeks her own agency by resisting her father's predations and refusing to participate in his fevered longings.

This theme of the bad father dominated Mary Shelley's work right from the beginning, even when it was concealed from the reader. *Six Weeks*, for example, does not appear to be a narrative about fathers, as parents are never mentioned, but hidden beneath the narrative is the story of her flight from her autocratic father. In 1814, Mary Shelley, Percy, and Claire did not simply set forth for Europe to enjoy an adventure. They fled England to escape Godwin's attempt to separate the young lovers. In 1816, when Godwin still refused to accept his daughter's relationship with Percy, they journeyed to Geneva to escape his critical eye. The reader can be forgiven for missing this theme, as at no point does Mary Shelley mention that their adventures stemmed from their attempt to free themselves from patriarchal restrictions. Nor does she recount any of the drama of that first flight: the secret decision to run away, the tiptoeing down the stairs, the note she propped on the mantelpiece for Godwin to read after she was gone, the pre-dawn departure, the frantic carriage ride from London, the overnight crossing to France, their pursuit by Mary Shelley's stepmother, Mary Jane, who found them in Calais and tried to persuade Claire to return home. Nevertheless, though Mary Shelley leaves all this unsaid, the book is still a testimonial to rebellion, still a story about three young people's revolt against parents. The 'vivacity' that *Blackwood's Edinburgh Magazine* noted in the writing stems in part from the triumphant quality of the narrative. Indeed, each joyful moment in *Six Weeks*, and even each distressing moment, becomes a symbol of the young people's hard-won freedom. They had wonderful adventures, Mary Shelley writes; and these adventures helped shape them into writers who were committed to liberal causes. Once they were released from parental tyranny, they poured themselves into their work, composing poems and novels for which they would one day become famous.

When considered together, these three early works explore the options of abused children: they can liberate themselves (*Six Weeks*), avenge themselves (*Frankenstein*), or separate themselves (*Mathilda*). When the father is either oppressive or dangerous, the children need to escape paternal tyranny, as the three young people do in *Six Weeks* and Mathilda does by separating herself from her father, envisioning a different world, free of horror, where flowers grow quietly in the grass, and new growth emerges from the grave. In *Frankenstein*, on the other hand, Victor's rejection of his 'son' leads to disaster. By abandoning the creature, he abandons his duties as a parent, leaving his 'child' to fend for himself in a world that treats him with cruelty. Ultimately, Mary Shelley makes it clear that Victor is to blame for the creature's violence. If Victor had been capable of parenting his 'son', she implies, the creature might never have given way to destructive rage.

In all three works, Mary Shelley depicts education as an important tool, but it has to be the right education. Both Victor and Mathilda's father receive little guidance when they are young. As a result, they never learn to check their impulses and the results are catastrophic for their children, demonstrating the generational impact of education, for good or ill. In *Six Weeks*, though, the opposite is true. The children break free and once they have escaped, they are liberated to learn from their own experiences and their own travels. To Mary Shelley, too much restraint is harmful, but so also is too little. The sweet spot is somewhere in the middle. And this is where mothers come in. The notable absence of female characters who can guide, nurture, and educate their children, lovers, and friends points to a theme that she would continue to develop in all of her work: the need for strong women who can contain the excesses of male passions and teach those around them how to live balanced lives based on good judgement, civility, and love.

Chapter 5
Valperga, The Last Man, The Fortunes of Perkin Warbeck, and the new *Frankenstein* (1821–1831)

Mary Shelley's middle novels, *Valperga*, *The Last Man*, and *The Fortunes of Perkin Warbeck*, are the first that she published under her own name. Although earlier female authors, such as Clara Reeve, Susannah Dobson, Ann Radcliffe, and Elizabeth Rowe, had attained acclaim for their work, ranging from translations and scholarly work to Gothic novels and historical fiction, it was still difficult for a woman author to make her way in what was essentially a man's world. The publication of work under her own name was always a significant step for any woman author, one that Jane Austen, for example, never took, and this made Mary Shelley's acknowledgement of her role as author particularly courageous as *Valperga*, *The Last Man*, and *The Fortunes of Perkin Warbeck* are more explicitly political than her earlier works (with the exception of *Six Weeks*). Developing some of the themes that she first articulated in *Six Weeks*, she depicts the evils of war and tyranny in all three novels, at the same time that she emphasizes the stumbling blocks that impede social and political reform. However, the dislocations in time and place in all three works allowed Mary Shelley to veil her critiques. Both *Valperga* and *Perkin Warbeck* are set in the past, enabling her to make her political points indirectly; she could describe the suffering caused by historical tyrants and long-ago wars, rather than detailing the problems caused by present-day rulers or contemporary conflicts. *The Last Man* also offers trenchant criticisms of 19th-century politics and social systems, but as a dystopian vision of a catastrophic future. For today's reader, Mary Shelley's political leanings are easily discernible. In the historical novels, the central female characters, Euthanasia and Catherine, articulate the Wollstonecraftian principles of freedom and community. Although they fail to achieve their goals, their advocacy is clearly meant to be admirable. In *The Last Man*, the protagonist Lionel supports and extends these ideas. One of the few male characters in Mary Shelley's fiction who is capable of growth and change, Lionel endures tremendous suffering, which gives him the wisdom he was lacking in his youth. Despite the overt political and ideological themes in all three of these books, most contemporary readers did not comment on them. Women writers were not, by convention, supposed to venture into the realm of politics, and so Mary Shelley's work was regularly misunderstood by reviewers. Critics characterized the historical novels *Valperga* and *Warbeck* as 'romances' and her apocalyptic vision of the future in *The Last Man* as 'diseased' and 'perverted', entirely overlooking her commitment to the radical themes of her mother.

Valperga (1823)

Mary Shelley's first historical novel *Valperga* took more than two years to write. Looking back, she said the idea came to her when she was still living in England, but she did not start writing the book until she had finished *Mathilda* in 1819, and had given birth to her fourth child, Percy Florence, in November of that same year. The new child's arrival could not, of course, take away from the grief of losing Clara or Wilmouse, but she relished having a child to nurture, writing to a friend that the five months of being childless, after Will's death, had been one of the most wrenching times in her life.

But though the new baby gave her a glimmer of hope, *Valperga* was still fuelled by the loss of her children and her increasing outrage over the repressive politics in England. That August, in what has become known as the Peterloo Massacre, cavalry charged into a crowd of around 60,000 people in Manchester who had gathered peacefully to demand greater representation in Parliament. The people's protests were well warranted. Poor economic conditions had created 'deep distress' amongst the working classes. According to one contemporary observer in Manchester, 'Nothing but ruin and starvation stare one in the face.' In Percy's sonnet 'England in 1819', the people are 'starved and stabbed in the untilled field'; the king is 'old, mad, blind, despised'. To Mary Shelley, of particular importance was the fact that of the 654 recorded casualties at Peterloo, at least 168 were women. Observers suggested that they were targeted by the soldiers, as they were easy to distinguish, dressed in the distinctive white of the reform movement. This violence amplified Mary Shelley's anger and she filled her new book with the principles of reform, once again using a historical setting to critique the problems she saw in her own time.

In Naples, before William died, she had begun to read medieval history as a way of coping with the loss of Clara. After she and Percy left Naples, she continued to delve into the past, researching and visiting historical sites. As part of her research, she came across the character of Prince Castruccio Castracani in a biography by Machiavelli. Machiavelli praises Castruccio for his ruthlessness as the leader of the Ghibellines in the civil war with the Guelphs in 14th-century Italy, but to Mary Shelley, who had never forgotten the devastated countryside in France, Castruccio seemed dangerous, the forerunner of a leader like Napoleon, charismatic but destructive, inspirational but tyrannical. She decided to write a novel based on his life, emphasizing the suffering he caused, condemning precisely what Machiavelli had admired, his strength as war commander and his bloodthirsty pursuit of power.

She began by tracing Castruccio's descent from innocent boy to cruel tyrant. Like the creature in *Frankenstein*, he does not start

Valperga

life as a murderous 'demon'; cruel treatment shapes him into a ruthless killer. Driven from his home by his family's enemies, he swears to avenge his loss. Old friends offer him refuge in Valperga, their castle, even though he is a Ghibelline and they are Guelphs. Here he is treated kindly by the Count, and falls in love with the Count's daughter, Euthanasia, a fictional character. A rational, self-aware, and classically educated young woman, Euthanasia's rigorous study of the Greeks and Romans has made her a proponent of natural liberties and republican government. Although it is highly unlikely that such a woman would have existed in 14th-century Tuscany, to Mary Shelley, historical accuracy was far less important than creating a female counterforce to Castruccio. She needed Euthanasia to reveal the impact of male ambition—war and oppressive acts of the state—on the lives of women as well as ordinary citizens. Furthermore, she subscribed to Romantic ideals about history writing, that readers needed the historical record to be enlivened by the imagination or they would find the past dry and lifeless.

Castruccio, inflamed with passion, pursues Euthanasia and she agrees to marry him—a hopeful moment in the narrative. Union between Castruccio and Euthanasia offers an opportunity for peace between the Guelphs and the Ghibellines. If they marry, they could unite the warring factions and harmony could rule the land. But Castruccio refuses to lay down his arms, impelled by his urge to conquer the land, including Euthanasia's Florence, and so Euthanasia breaks off their engagement, taking a stand for the liberty of her people. No matter how much she loves Castruccio, freedom is more important, she declares, refusing to let him dominate her or her people. With this heroic stance, Euthanasia becomes a champion of peace and liberty as well as the leader of the forces who try to stop the prince. Ultimately, she fails, as Castruccio quickly subdues the Guelph strongholds, burning down Euthanasia's home, Valperga. After her defeat, Castruccio exiles Euthanasia to Sicily. During the voyage, her ship sinks and she drowns.

Euthanasia's death at the end of the novel belies her strength as a character and seems, at first, a pessimistic ending. But even though she loses the struggle with Castruccio, Euthanasia offers a significant alternative to the ambitions of the warlord. An active and inspirational leader, she challenges his power—a challenge that is absent in *Frankenstein*, where no one except the creature can do battle with Victor. Accordingly, the narrator's claim that 'Earth felt no change when she died; and men forgot her' is undercut by the novel itself, as, far from being forgotten when she dies, Euthanasia, fictional creation though she is, lives on in the pages of *Valperga*. The narrative becomes a restoration, even a resurrection of a heroic woman's life. In 'returning' Euthanasia's story to history, Mary Shelley undermines the glorification of war and subverts Machiavelli's version of Castruccio as a hero, presenting Castruccio's wars of conquest as villainous acts of destruction. As Euthanasia laments, the people are driven from their homes, 'often a poor child lost, or haplessly wounded, whose every drop of blood is of more worth than the power of the Caesars'.

If Castruccio symbolizes the dangerous effects of male ambition and is blinded by his obsessive need to avenge the miseries of his childhood, Euthanasia stands for enlightened reform, peace, union, harmony, and reason—the virtues which Wollstonecraft had advocated, and which all of the male characters in Mary Shelley's fiction had hitherto resisted or undercut. Euthanasia is forward thinking and dreams of a united Italy, just as Mary Shelley and her fellow reformers dreamed of a united Europe in the aftermath of the Napoleonic wars. Although her hopes that the national leaders at the Congress of Vienna would embrace liberal reforms were dashed, the dream of a unified Europe predicated on natural rights would continue to inspire Mary Shelley for the rest of her career.

Euthanasia's unusual name points to Mary Shelley's political ideals. Angela Wright explains that 'Euthanasia' means 'good death' or 'noble death', and is probably derived from Mary Shelley's reading of Hume's *Essays, Moral and Political* in which Hume writes that absolute monarchy is 'the easiest death, the true euthanasia of the British constitution'. By creating the character of Euthanasia, Mary Shelley could write a story where the tyrant has a worthy opponent, a strong woman who leads the fight against injustice. But Euthanasia's death is also essential to the story, as Mary Shelley wanted to demonstrate that when men are guided by ambition, not love, and by fame not family, then not only do women and children pay the price, but so does all of humanity. Euthanasia's many virtues cannot triumph over Castruccio's lust for power, but her memory can live on as an inspiration for freedom fighters everywhere.

Midway through the novel, Mary Shelley introduces a second female character, Beatrice, whose tragic fate reinforces the idea that war and conquest cause suffering. Beatrice, the daughter of Wilhelmina, a historical figure from the 12th century, whose followers saw her as the Holy Ghost, the saviour of the female sex, is another of Mary Shelley's inventions. Like Wilhelmina, she is viewed as a saviour by her followers, but she is persecuted by the Inquisition. She escapes, with the help of sympathetic priests, only to fall in love with Castruccio. Unlike Euthanasia, she does not have the benefit of a rational education, and, as a result, is not independent enough to withstand his passion. Having been raised in the 'superstitions' of the church, she is at the mercy of her feelings and dreams. Unable to recognize Castruccio's capacity for cruelty, she surrenders to him completely, losing her sense of self. When he casts her off, she is captured by a villainous priest who imprisons her and rapes her.

The virtuous Euthanasia rescues Beatrice from her sufferings, even though she knows that Beatrice is in love with Castruccio. In a traditional romance, they would have been pitted against each other as opponents, but in Mary Shelley's novel, their friendship triumphs over their feelings for Castruccio. Indeed, that their love stories with Castruccio fail is one of the most significant points of the novel. As a character, Castruccio is too self-enclosed, and too much of a tyrant, to allow either woman to sway him from his bloody course. Euthanasia's appeal to reason and peace cannot restrain him, and neither can Beatrice's beauty and mysticism.

Drawn together by their sufferings and the truths they have come to understand, both women are protective of each other. Although Beatrice is not as strong as Euthanasia and cannot rescue her from Castruccio, she can take care of her in other ways. Accordingly, as Angela Wright points out, when Euthanasia asks Beatrice to tell her about the tortures she has endured, Beatrice gives her an edited version to spare Euthanasia pain. Like Mathilda, she refuses to obsess over the abuse she has experienced, exerting control over her narrative and differentiating herself from Victor Frankenstein and Walton, who recite the terrors they have experienced in gruesome detail, knowing full well that they will induce 'blood curdling' horror in their listeners.

Euthanasia records Beatrice's tale as well as her own, stories that would otherwise go untold. Like her creator, and like Mathilda, Euthanasia is a writer, as her 'private chronicles' are the purported origins of *Valperga*. Through the miracle of fiction, Mary Shelley has 'remembered her', keeping alive not only Euthanasia's particular story but the story of Beatrice, the story of two women who support one another in the midst of oppression.

With the creation of these two female characters, and the allusion to Wilhelmina, Mary Shelley invokes her mother's ideals, setting them against the militaristic values of Machiavelli and his successors. Although Beatrice is represented as a weaker character, she and her mother are still important figures, as they demonstrate Mary Shelley's view that the church's patriarchal system abused women and deprived them of power. Having been trained to devote herself to her mystical dreams, and obey the dictates of her overly active imagination, Beatrice is not capable of

Euthanasia's reasoned approach to life, but she is still able to forge a bond with Euthanasia—a far stronger alliance than either woman can have with the 'great' warlord. Ultimately, by making Euthanasia and Beatrice central characters in the novel, Mary Shelley was able to augment, comment on, and cast doubt on the historical record. Fiction was the only way to include the perspectives of women, whose voices were traditionally absent from chronicles and archives.

When *Valperga* was published, Mary Shelley expected to be attacked for her radical politics, embedded as they were in the women's viewpoints, but the reviewers missed the ideas that inspired the novel: the novel's critique of tyranny, its advocacy for reform, its celebration of female friendship and education, and its depiction of Euthanasia as a fearless leader who defies the authoritarian desires of a warlord. Instead, they commented on Euthanasia as a feminine ideal of virtue and criticized the author for having Euthanasia reject Castruccio. As the reviewer in the *Literary Gazette* declared, 'It scarcely seems in woman's nature for patriotism to be a stronger feeling than love.' Nor did they praise Mary Shelley's innovations, how she had overturned the conventions of the historical romance by creating two heroines who forge an alliance against 'the hero', who is, in fact, a villain.

But in fact, in Castruccio, Mary Shelley had created another monstrous character, this time handsome in appearance, but monstrous all the same—a domineering male figure who killed children, as the creature did in *Frankenstein*. And she had also created a heroine, a female adversary, who may not have been able to prevent her opponent's military victories, but who could represent another way, another course to history. Through fiction, Mary Shelley was able to offer a critique of the historical account, as well as a critique of male 'heroism'. Mary Shelley had come far from *Frankenstein*. Though Euthanasia cannot stop Castruccio's aggression, Mary Shelley emphasizes her importance in the narrative, setting Castruccio's politics of war against Euthanasia's politics of reason, his politics of violence against her politics of peace. Even the ending, which, as the scholar Betty T. Bennett argues, is 'open' and 'cyclical', rather than conclusive, suggests that history moves in waves, and that no act of protest is for naught. Accordingly, though Castruccio triumphs over Euthanasia in this particular moment of history, Mary Shelley emphasizes that his victory is temporary. He, too, dies, and his kingdom falls, opening the door for another wave of resistance, another chance at reform, another Euthanasia, who might succeed.

Ultimately, *Valperga* represents a remarkable departure from Mary Shelley's first two novels. In the dystopian world of *Frankenstein*, the strongest female character, MWS, is offstage and the other women (with the exception of Safie) are murdered. Even the female creature who could have had a positive influence on the creature is destroyed by Victor. In *Mathilda*, the heroine is capable of resisting her father, but her life is both limited and defined by him. Not until *Valperga* did Mary envision a female character who could stand up to a tyrant. Euthanasia may lose her battle with Castruccio, but Castruccio's tyranny and cruelty earns him the condemnation of history, while Euthanasia's courage, integrity, and commitment to peace and liberty serve as inspiration. Furthermore, *Valperga* is one of the first novels to demonstrate the suffering caused by Machiavelli's political philosophy. Others had condemned Machiavelli's means-to-an-end policies, but Mary Shelley explored their real-life consequences, the cruelties of this kind of leadership. Castruccio betrays those he loves to consolidate his empire. He is treacherous, killing opponents without mercy. Like Victor Frankenstein, he has boundless ambition, pursuing 'honor, fame, dominion', despite his beloved's protests. In Euthanasia, on the other hand, Mary Shelley had created a standard bearer for freedom, a woman who could show protesters how to persevere in the face of tyranny, who refused marriage to fight for freedom. An embodiment of Wollstonecraft's principles, Euthanasia is an emblem of the possibilities of radical reform.

As Mary Shelley put the finishing touches to *Valperga*, news arrived that served to confirm her bleak outlook on the world. The newly crowned English king, George IV, whom she and other liberals despised as an authoritarian fool, had driven his wife, Queen Caroline, out of England simply because he disliked her. If the queen, whom Mary Shelley admired for being the symbolic leader of the liberal movement in England, could be sent into exile on the whim of her husband, it was further evidence of how all women, even queens, were at the mercy of men, and how liberty was the victim of tyranny. The world needed her novel, she believed. She needed to continue the fight that her mother began in *A Vindication of the Rights of Woman*. Not just for the rights of woman, but for the rights of all people. It was her duty to be a kind of literary Euthanasia and use her writing to advance the causes of reform, education, peace, and independence.

Percy's death

But Mary Shelley's life was about to undergo a dramatic change. In 1822, after she had sent the manuscript of *Valperga* to England for publication, tragedy struck again. This time it would overturn everything, setting her on a path she could never have envisioned.

After the deaths of Clara and Wilmouse, Mary Shelley and Percy had become increasingly estranged. When Percy Florence was born, Mary Shelley had retreated almost entirely into the writing of *Valperga*, while Percy involved himself in his own projects and, most likely, had affairs with other women. They were still each other's first readers for their work, but Mary Shelley felt that Percy did not mourn their children deeply enough. Percy believed that she was too hard on him and complained to his friends that she was cold and critical. The tension between them slowly mounted, until it came to a sudden end on 8 July 1822.

That summer, Mary Shelley, Claire, and Percy had retreated from the heat of Pisa, where they had been living, to the Bay of Spezia with their friends Jane and Edward Williams. Byron, too, had found a house further down the coast. Pregnant for the fifth time, Mary Shelley wrote to her friend Maria Gisborne, 'My nerves were wound up to the utmost irritation.... No words can tell you how I hated our house and the country about it.'

This house, the Casa Magni, was a big wedge-shaped villa with dirty white walls, isolated from the tiny town by a stony beach and steep hill (Figure 7).

Originally a boathouse, the Casa Magni opened to the sea. Sometimes, the water washed over the small stone wall, flooding the ground floor, thrilling Percy and horrifying Mary Shelley. There was no escaping the pounding of the surf. It was impossible to walk to town in the heat, especially if one was tired and pregnant. But everything that Mary Shelley loathed, Percy loved: the isolation, the bleak coastal scenery, the loneliness of the location. He could not swim, but was passionate about sailing and had hired a new friend, Edward Trelawny, who had retired from the navy, to oversee the building of a new boat. When the boat was delivered to the Casa Magni, Percy was as delighted as a small child. He christened her the *Ariel*, and spent most of his time tinkering with the rigging, sailing, or, leaning against the mast,

7. **The Casa Magni.**

jotting down ideas for poems in his notebook. But his spirits sank when Byron came sailing into the Bay, as Byron's ship was bigger and faster. Always competitive with Byron, he devised a plan to lengthen the masts of his boat. More experienced sailors would have known that the *Ariel* did not have a deep enough keel to handle bigger sails, but Percy only cared about making his boat swifter than Byron's.

Mary Shelley watched these proceedings with foreboding. But she was feeling increasingly ill and on 16 June woke up bleeding. Percy came to the rescue, plunging her into an ice bath and saving her life, but she lost the child—another loss, another sorrow to add to the others. For days, she was too weak to get up. She begged Percy to stay with her, but he was restless, and insisted on sailing across the gulf to visit Byron, ostensibly to discuss their new literary journal, the *Liberal*, which Percy had started with Byron and other friends, but also to show off the improvements to his new boat.

Mary Shelley and Jane Williams watched their husbands set sail on 1 July. Later, Mary Shelley wrote that she could hardly 'endure' that he had left and 'cried bitterly when he went away'. Percy promised they would sail back in a week, but 8 July came and went and the men did not return. As the days passed, it became clear that something had happened. At last, on 19 July, news came that the bodies of Percy, Edward Williams, and an 18-year-old boy whom they had hired as an extra hand had washed up on shore. Apparently, a storm had blown up on the 8th when the sailors were about 10 miles out to sea, at least four hours away from the protected waters near Casa Magni. Although no one blamed him for the ship's poor design, Trelawny seems to have felt guilty, as he created a false story, saying that pirates had attacked Percy and Edward Williams. But this story has never been substantiated and seems to have stemmed from Trelawny's desire to evade responsibility, as one of the reasons the ship went down was its general unseaworthiness.

Too heartbroken to oversee the details of the burial, Mary Shelley allowed Trelawny to organize a theatrical send-off. He arranged a funeral pyre for both men, burning Edward Williams on 15 August and Percy on 16 August. Mary Shelley could not bear to witness this event, evidence to Trelawny that she was not worthy of Percy's love, but even Byron could not bear to watch, leaving Trelawny alone at the fire, convincing him that, though he had just met Percy the preceding year, he was actually Percy's truest friend. As Percy's corpse 'fell open', Trelawny later recalled, 'the heart was laid bare'. He snatched it from the flames and gave it to Percy's friend Leigh Hunt, as he thought that Mary Shelley did not seem grief stricken enough to warrant having the heart. But Mary Shelley's way of coping with sorrow had always been to retreat into herself, appearing unmoved to those who did not know her well. In her journal, she addressed the accusations of those who accused her of being unfeeling, 'A cold heart! Have I a cold heart? God knows!…at least the tears are hot.' Fortunately, Jane Williams intervened, asking Hunt to give the heart to Mary Shelley, and he agreed. However, this battle was a sign of what was to come, as Trelawny would go on to publish his criticisms of Mary Shelley in his memoir. The two sparred over the publication of Percy's poetry and other issues, none of which would matter to history if Trelawny's negative opinions had not harmed Mary Shelley's reputation after she died.

Unaware of Trelawny's machinations, Mary Shelley was devastated and guilt-ridden. She had been cold to Percy in the weeks before his death, and angry. Now, she could not forgive herself. 'All that might have been bright in my life is now despoiled,' she wrote to her friend Maria Gisborne on 15 August. At the age of 24, Mary Shelley was a widow. She had one surviving little boy. Heartbroken, she decided to compensate for her treatment of Percy by dedicating her life to publishing his work and telling his life story. But pragmatic concerns interrupted her plans. After Percy's death, his allowance from his father, Sir Timothy, came to an abrupt halt. Before she could write his biography and publish his poems, she needed an income, and so she sought to augment her finances, publishing 'A Tale of the Passions', and two biographical essays, in the *Liberal*. *Valperga* was published in 1823, along with another edition of *Frankenstein*, but these publications did not bring in much money, and so, with reluctance, she wrote to Sir Timothy, asking for assistance.

This was a difficult letter to write, as she knew that Sir Timothy hated her. He had been her implacable enemy ever since she ran away with Percy, even going to court in an attempt to invalidate their marriage. She hoped that the thought of his grandson would soften his heart, but Sir Timothy refused to help her unless she returned to England and handed her son over to the Shelley family. She refused to surrender Percy Florence, but she did return to London, where Sir Timothy remained adamant; he would provide no financial support unless he had the boy. But Mary Shelley, who had already lost three children and had just completed a novel imagining a female character's brave resistance to male tyranny, was, like Euthanasia, a worthy opponent, and hired an excellent lawyer. In November 1823, she won a small allowance from the Shelley estate, but in exchange she had to agree not to publish any of Percy's works or write anything about him. If she disregarded these rules, she would be cut off without a penny. Furthermore, if Sir Timothy discovered that she was in debt and could not support herself and her son, then he would take her child into custody—Mary Shelley's greatest fear.

Sir Timothy's allowance was helpful, but it was not enough to free Mary Shelley from the need to earn money and she realized that she would have to stay in England to be close to the publishing world. Other women writers, including her mother, had earned enough money to support themselves, but she knew it would be an uphill battle. She wrote in her journal that she felt 'unprotected', and even attacked, as women were not supposed to live independently in conservative English society. She missed her old life, ensconced in the world of Percy, Byron, and other friends who shared the same liberal values. But she knew she had to work in order to survive and began turning out stories and articles with remarkable efficiency. Her father, whom Percy had supported for years, made it clear that he expected her to continue to assist him, and so she wrote for outlets that paid well, giving Godwin as much of her earnings as she could afford. The irony of Godwin's insistence that his daughter, a single mother, support him, a long-established novelist and political philosopher, was entirely lost on him (and on her). To Godwin, his own writing was of such monumental importance that nothing should stand in its way, particularly money. Mary Shelley, who had been taught to revere him, agreed; for the good of the world, her father's writing had to be encouraged, fostered, and supported.

Even though she struggled to make enough to support herself and her family, her reputation as a writer was growing. While she was abroad, *Frankenstein* had been adapted for the stage and became popular with theatregoers. When she attended a production at the Lyceum Theatre, protesters marched outside, bearing placards condemning the play, but they could not stop the crowds from filing into the theatre. Proud that so many had come to see her story staged, Mary Shelley wrote to a friend that she had 'become famous'. The irony is that she earned nothing from this production, nor from any of the others based on her book. In 19th-century England, playwrights were allowed to borrow from novels without crediting the author. They were also under no obligation to be faithful to the original story. Stage versions of *Frankenstein* tended to simplify the plot, making Mary Shelley's multifaceted creature a pure villain, rather than the complex mix of abandoned child and vengeful murderer she had created. Another odd development was that over time, Mary Shelley's hubristic Victor Frankenstein almost entirely disappeared from public awareness. By as early as the 1840s, the word Frankenstein had become synonymous with the monster, and Mary Shelley's name became associated with that of a murderous fiend.

At length, after establishing herself as a reliable writer for various monthlies, Mary Shelley decided to defy Sir Timothy's directive and produce a volume of Percy's work anonymously. She approached this project with eagerness, though it was far more complicated than it initially seemed. Percy had never been a tidy person and his papers were in disarray. He had written on scraps of paper and the backs of envelopes. Many poems had been composed on different sheets of paper, making it difficult to tell where new poems began and old ones ended. Those poems that were written on one piece of paper were obscured by doodles of trees and sailboats.

For Mary Shelley, going through Percy's papers was a bittersweet process. It gave her the sense that they were still in communication, but it also brought home his absence. Miserable though she was, she made the additions and deletions he seemed to indicate, choosing final versions and piecing together lines written in different locations. Fortunately, for the most part, she was working with material she had seen before. She and Percy had talked about most of the drafts, collaborators to the end. But there were also poems that Mary saw for the first time. Many of these lamented her absence from his life and his loneliness, or praised other women at her expense. As difficult as these were to read, Mary Shelley wanted the public to see his best work, and, with admirable selflessness, included these poems as well.

She spent six months working on his papers, creating one of her most significant and most unsung accomplishments: a coherent collection of Shelley's work, a volume that would never have existed without her efforts. She wrote an anonymous preface, praising Percy as an ethereal spirit and an artist. Although she was clear that he had 'fearless enthusiasm' for 'the moral and physical state of mankind' and that this was why he was 'pursued by hatred' in his lifetime, she left out all direct mention of his notorious radicalism, his atheism, and his calls for political reform. In part this was to make his work more appealing to the public, but it was also an effort to appease Sir Timothy.

In June 1824 she published 500 copies of *Posthumous Poems*. The book sold briskly until Sir Timothy heard about it. He could not prove it, but he knew who was behind its publication and forced the publisher to recall all the unsold copies. However, he was too late to stop Mary Shelley's vision of Percy from reaching the public. The book was widely shared among friends and Percy's reputation as a poet began to grow, as did a new version of the poet: Percy, the gentle soul, too good for this harsh world.

The Last Man (1826)

While Mary Shelley was working on *Posthumous Poems*, she received yet more disastrous news. Byron had died of malaria in Greece, where he had been fighting in the War of Independence from the Ottoman Empire. The English clergy refused to bury him in Westminster, and so he was laid to rest in the family vault near Newstead. Mary Shelley watched the funeral procession from the window of the cottage she was renting. To her it seemed the end of an era. In her journal, she wrote that she was 'a survivor. The Last Man! Yes, I may well describe that solitary being's feelings, feeling myself as the last relic of a beloved race, my companions extinct before me.' Inspired as it was by grief and heartbreak, Mary Shelley's next book dramatized the words of her journal—*The Last Man*.

After the losses she had sustained and the dramatic changes in her life, Mary Shelley's aims were broader than in *Valperga*. She was still preoccupied with the principles of reform, but she wanted to go further and write about the shattering of the world, her sense that humankind was on the brink of extinction. In the preface, she writes that she has deciphered the tale from words traced on 'leaves' that she and 'a friend' discovered in Naples, in the cave of the Cumaean Sibyl, a cave that she and Percy did in fact visit. By declaring that she is the one who has written down this story, she links herself to her very first book, *Six Weeks*, which she edited and wrote largely on her own, and the female editors of her previous novels, Margaret Saville Walton, Mathilda, and

Euthanasia, who are all the organizers and preservers of the stories they tell.

This authorial intrusion is the only moment Mary Shelley enters the story, but it is an important moment. On the one hand, the 'discovery' of the leaves is as much a fiction as the tale she sets out to tell, but it is also useful preparation for the imaginative flight to come, as the novel is set far in the future, beginning in 2073 and ending in 2100, tracing the course of a global pandemic that ultimately kills everyone except the narrator, Lionel Verney. Mary Shelley had explored the idea of authorial intrusion a few years before in 'Giovanni Villani', one of the essays she had written for the *Liberal* right after Percy died. In this work, she explains that sometimes when the author speaks directly to the reader, 'a chord' could be awakened, which otherwise might have gone unheard. In another essay from the same time period, 'On Ghosts', she argues that setting and atmosphere are essential elements when creating the supernatural in fiction. To demonstrate her point, she includes her own experience of mourning a 'lost friend' (Percy) and visiting the last house where she had seen him. Interestingly, she spends more time describing the house itself than her encounter with his spirit. Only at the end of the passage does she say, 'me thought, I heard, I felt—I know not what—but I trembled'.

In *The Last Man*, though, when Mary Shelley announces her identity as the 'editor', she does this not only to establish the novel's futuristic setting but to assert her authority over the narrative, claiming that the leaves were so difficult to read that there would have been no story without her efforts. It is she, therefore, who is the invisible hand behind Lionel's narrative, and though she does not re-enter the story, her mark on the novel is clear. She has framed it as 'her' story, as much if not more than the narrator's—her first and only such assertion as a novelist.

When *The Last Man* begins, it appears to follow the same trajectory as *Frankenstein* and *Valperga*. Like Castruccio and the creature in *Frankenstein*, Lionel is angry and dreams of revenge for wrongs that were done to his family. But unlike the earlier characters, he undergoes a conversion. He has sworn to hate Adrian, the crown prince whom he believes has harmed his family, but when they meet, Lionel is inspired by Adrian's idealism. Modelled on Percy, Adrian embodies many of the poet's virtues and political dreams. He renounces the throne, in an attempt to turn England into the republic of Mary Shelley's dreams. Lionel, inspired by Adrian's commitment to justice, learns to follow Adrian's lead and devote himself to others. But over time, he also learns that Adrian is sometimes too idealistic. Occasionally, he loses sight of reality when his dreams and visions overpower him.

Another important male character, Lord Raymond, offers a counterpoint to Adrian. Modelled after Byron, Raymond is an ambitious nobleman, who achieves fame by helping the Greeks win independence from the Turks. In contrast to Adrian, Raymond dreams of power, but he restrains himself for a time because he is in love with Lionel's sister and marries her. The friends enjoy a peaceful sojourn in the countryside, but instead of following philosophical principles like Adrian, Raymond is impulsive and emotional, and this will be his undoing. As the monarchy has been abolished, he becomes instead the Lord Protector of England and then returns to the war in Greece, where he dies in an explosion, the result of a trap laid by the Turks.

There are many other subplots that run throughout the novel, but the second half of the book focuses on the progress of the pandemic, which spreads rapidly across Europe and America. Survivors from America plunder Ireland, Scotland, and England. The weather becomes apocalyptic. A black sun causes panic. Seacoast towns are flooded by storm surges. In France, a false messiah rises up, leading followers in a strange fanatical cult. Lionel and Adrian and their friends escape for a time to Switzerland, but when the disease finds them there, they sail to Greece; however, a sudden storm sinks their ship, drowning

Adrian. Lionel escapes by swimming to shore, landing on the beach in Ravenna, where he finds no one else alive. He follows the road to Rome, his only companion a sheepdog he finds along the way.

The city is empty when he arrives, and he contents himself with spending a year alone in Rome, musing over the fate of civilization, saddened but still fully sane, having endured more pain than he could have imagined when he was young. Over the course of the novel, he has learned to reject the extremes of both Adrian and Raymond. He is idealistic like Adrian, but is still able to grasp reality; he is moved by emotions like Raymond, but still has control over his actions. Accordingly, he does not rage at his fate. Nor is he deluded by his dreams or wishes. Instead he weeps as he faces the reality of his situation, able to experience grief instead of anger, unlike the male characters in Mary Shelley's previous novels, or even his younger self. At first, he feels self-conscious for being 'girlish', but, ultimately, he embraces his capacity to have deep and authentic feelings, having become more like Euthanasia than Castruccio. Suffering has transformed him and redeemed him; the conventional boundaries between male and female have blurred, and he sets sail to find another survivor across the sea.

For all its horrific (and prescient) vision of the future, *The Last Man* suggests the possibility of growth and change, a possibility that is lacking in Mary Shelley's earlier works, where the male characters cannot be swayed from their paths. Lionel survives, she suggests, because he is the one character who has allowed himself to evolve. Early on, he drops his revenge fantasies—an impossibility for Castruccio, Frankenstein, and his creature—and learns to experience sorrow instead of rage, containing the horror of the apocalypse by writing down his story, just as Mary Shelley's other 'survivors' had. Unlike her earlier characters, who are all women, Lionel is able to have a future: Mathilda commits suicide, Euthanasia drowns, and MWS's fate is unknown, but Lionel sets forth on a quest. Of course, in such a bleak novel, it is difficult to see this as a bright moment, and yet, Lionel's wisdom at the end of the novel is hopeful. He has attained a reasoned viewpoint and an ethical stance on the disaster that has struck the world. 'A solitary being is by instinct a wanderer,' he reflects, as he prepares to leave Rome. 'I shall witness all the variety of appearance, that the elements can assume—I shall read fair augury in the rainbow—menace in the cloud—some lesson or record dear to my heart in everything.' In the end, after what he has experienced, he declares that he will be able to read all the signs of the world.

When *The Last Man* was published in January 1826, the response was overwhelmingly negative. Critics complained that Mary Shelley's writing was too dark. In an era that celebrated progress *The Last Man*'s pessimism struck a discordant note. Humankind was on the brink of calamity, Mary Shelley implied, leading pundits to wonder what kind of woman had dreamed up this nightmare vision. Sir Timothy was so horrified that he withheld Mary Shelley's allowance, but she fought back, hiring her lawyer to force him to resume payments. Although there were a few positive responses—the artist John Martin painted a series of works inspired by the novel, 'An Ideal Design of The Last Man', and the book was translated into French—she was disheartened by its poor sales, and promised her publisher that her next book would be more popular.

Though downcast by the novel's sales, Mary Shelley did not abandon her reformist ideals. Instead, she applied her philosophy to her life, tackling hypocrisy and suffering by spending her money and her time helping her women friends. The virtues of her ideal female character, Euthanasia, were the virtues she wanted to uphold in her own life: integrity, balance, empathy, reason, courage, and common sense. Accordingly, she helped a dear friend 'elope' with another woman to Europe. Nineteen-year-old Isabel Robinson had had a baby out of wedlock and confided in Mary Shelley that if her father discovered this, he would cast her out of

Valperga

the house. Mary Shelley's friend, Mary Diana Dods—'Doddy'—who was notorious for her affairs with women, was in love with Isabel and so Mary Shelley and Doddy conceived of a plan where Doddy would pose as a man and set off for France with Isabel. Once there, they would pretend to be man and wife. After a few years, Doddy would fade away and Isabel could go back home to England, a respectable widow with a child. It was an absurd plan, and if they were caught, they would all face disgrace, but Mary Shelley was her mother's daughter, and so she assumed the role of mastermind. At the end of the summer, Isabel and Doddy moved to France and a few years later Isabel returned to England with her daughter. No one was ever the wiser. Mary Shelley also gave financial assistance to many other women friends, including Jane, the widow of Percy's friend Edward Williams, and Claire. She gave advice and counsel to the young women in her social circle and beyond, befriending those who were cast out for 'immorality' or other social infractions.

The Fortunes of Perkin Warbeck (1830)

The Last Man did not earn enough money to support Mary Shelley and Percy Florence. Godwin, too, continued to need her financial support, and so Mary Shelley persevered by writing stories for magazines. The audience for these was primarily women and many of the stories echo the themes of her novels: power, male ambition, female righteousness, love, the supernatural, ghosts, and the imagination. The most notable of these—'A Tale of the Passions', 'The Brother and Sister', 'The Heir of Mondolfo', 'The Dream', 'The Mortal Immortal', and 'Transformation'—demonstrate her continued commitment to expanding the range of the Gothic to include ideas of radical political and social reform, as well as a celebration of the imagination and the dignity of women. In 'Transformation', for example, she appears at first to be writing a Gothic tale about Guido, a selfish young man who trades places with a dwarf for the sake of hedonistic pleasure, but becomes trapped in the dwarf's body. In a more conventional tale, like Charles Robert Maturin's *Melmoth the Wanderer*, the central character would be damned forever. But Mary Shelley adds a characteristic edge to the story, by allowing Guido to find the dwarf, return to his own form, and marry his true love, Juliet. Juliet, however, does not accept him back as though nothing had happened. Guido tells the reader that Juliet 'sometimes ventures to allude bitterly to the malice that caused this change', suggesting that although he has returned, his mistake has not vanished from the record. Juliet has not forgotten, and she will not let him forget either.

In 1829, Mary Shelley also lent secret support to a new publication of Percy's work, giving editorial assistance and providing some biographical details. She was glad to see his poetry gaining a readership, but she still yearned to write his biography and to bring out a complete edition of his work. However, since Sir Timothy's restrictions still held her back, she turned to fiction, setting her new novel, *The Fortunes of Perkin Warbeck*, in the 15th century, once again embedding her radical messages in history.

As in *Valperga*, she felt no need to stay true to historical events, shaping the characters and backdrop to suit her own ends. In the preface she says that 'facts' are not enough to 'do justice' to the story. As the critic Erin L. W. Garret argues, she uses fiction to critique the historical record. The real Perkin Warbeck was a pretender to the English throne, who claimed to be the escaped Richard, Duke of York, the second son of King Edward IV, one of the little princes who had been imprisoned in the Tower. In Mary Shelley's novel, Perkin is who he says he is, Richard, the inheritor of the throne. But though she depicts Richard as idealistic and empathic, a good and virtuous man, he is not the hero of her tale. Neither is Henry VII, his opponent, whom she depicts as power-hungry and villainous. Rather, it is Katherine Gordon, Richard's wife, a real historical figure, whom Mary Shelley reimagines as the true beacon of light in the novel. The war over the throne is causing suffering to the people, Katherine declares, fighting against Richard's ambition, just as Euthanasia had resisted Castruccio. Also, like Euthanasia, she argues on behalf of peace. It is not war that will improve the condition of humankind, she says. What really matter are harmony and love, the embracing of rational and domestic values, and the creation of a 'sentimental community' for those who have 'fellow feeling with the oppressed' as Mary Shelley had first envisioned in *Six Weeks* and which she would continue to develop in her final novels.

As Betty T. Bennett has explained, when *Perkin Warbeck* was published in 1830, contemporary critics ignored the radical anti-war message, just as they had with *Valperga*, overlooking the republican politics embedded in the plot. The *New Monthly Magazine* praised the novel's 'feminine delicacy of feeling' and its 'peculiar charm'. Although these were comparatively positive reviews for a novel by Mary Shelley, she was still disappointed at how, once again, reviewers had missed the central points. Some 20th-century critics disliked the novel for the opposite reason, viewing it as not political enough. To them, Katherine Gordon's anti-war and anti-monarchal views were problematic, as they signalled a retreat from the public to the private realm, and a prioritization of the domestic sphere over the political.

But both readings of the novel misrepresent Mary Shelley's aims as an author, particularly as a female writer committed to advancing the cause of women. One of the most important innovations of *Perkin Warbeck* is that Mary Shelley gives Katherine Gordon her own voice. She calls attention to this by including a footnote where she writes, 'the character of the Lady Katherine Gordon is a favorite of mine ... I desired therefore that she speak for herself.' Mary Shelley's editorial remarks underline the centrality of both the female author and her female protagonist. When Katherine speaks, she argues for liberty in the face of tyranny. To her, it is the fight for power that causes suffering for the people, and she argues for peace. But, of course, these are Mary Shelley's words, as she had to invent Katherine's speeches. The chronicles of this time period rarely include accounts of women, even of queens. As Erin Webster concludes, Mary Shelley's blend of fiction and fact makes the novel a 'revisionary history'. Without the devices of fiction, she would not have been able to give Katherine Gordon a voice.

Mary Shelley's politics are further illustrated by the letters she wrote during the same year that she published *Perkin Warbeck*. Still an avid follower of international politics, she was heartened to read that General Lafayette was promoting reform in France, and wrote him a letter, praising his proposals. To friends, she wrote that the wealthy in England needed to sacrifice their own riches, rather than taxing the poor. Most interesting of all, she wrote to the publisher John Murray proposing two book ideas: first, a 'History of Woman' and second, a 'Lives of Celebrated Women'. Murray declined these proposals, but they demonstrate Mary Shelley's ambition to make the lives of women her central focus.

Surprisingly, there was a positive side to the critical misunderstanding of Mary Shelley's work. Although she was still regarded as a scandalous figure by the old guard, she had attained a literary stature that had seemed unattainable when she was the 20-year-old anonymous author of *Frankenstein*. In 1830, the *Athenaeum* declared that she was the most distinguished literary woman of her time and the publisher Bentley offered Mary Shelley a place on its list for *Frankenstein* if she revised it so that they could own the copyright.

The new *Frankenstein* (1831)

Mary Shelley embraced the opportunity to rethink her first novel. The tragedies she had endured had taken their toll, and in this new version of her book she painted an even bleaker picture of the world than in the original. In the first edition, Victor has at least some freedom to choose whether to pursue his ambitions. When he makes the wrong choice, it is his own action that brings about his downfall. But in this new version, Mary Shelley strips him of any agency. He is a puppet in the hands of inexorable forces, a man who must obey his impulses. Elizabeth, too, has far less independence. She is now an orphan instead of Victor's cousin, a change in status that reinforces her weakness, as she has no family of her own. Victor's mother gives her to Victor as a 'pretty present' and for the remainder of the story, she is his to dispose of at will. By diminishing Elizabeth, Mary Shelley demonstrated the danger of depriving women of their independence. Without a Katherine Gordon or a Euthanasia to fight against the destructive force of male ambitions, everyone in the novel suffers.

On another note, as the scholar Susan Wolfson argues, by making Elizabeth an orphan, Mary Shelley can show how her adoption by the Frankenstein family is 'racially inflected'. Many scholars have pointed to Mary Shelley's stance against slavery in the first edition, arguing that the creature's hardships are based, in part, on the slave narratives Mary Shelley had read. But in this new edition, Mary Shelley goes further, painting an even more disturbing picture of the consequences of racism by emphasizing the harm done by the prejudices of the central characters. Victor's mother discovers the blonde Elizabeth when she passes by a 'dark-eyed' peasant family who have adopted the orphan child. Immediately, Mrs Frankenstein wants to take Elizabeth away and raise her as her own. Mary Shelley emphasizes the child's whiteness, writing that Elizabeth's hair is golden and that she is 'fairer than a garden rose among dark leaved brambles', making it clear that it is her fair (white) skin and 'golden' hair that attract Mrs Frankenstein. In contrast, the other 'orphan' in the story is neglected and abandoned. No one wants to 'adopt' Frankenstein's abandoned creature because of his ugliness—an ugliness that many critics view as racially coded. For instance, Mary Shelley describes the creature's lips and hair as 'black' and his skin as 'yellow'. John Malchow suggests that Mary Shelley's depiction is based on her society's 'general image of the "Negro" body in which repulsive features, brute-like strength and size of limbs featured prominently'. Karen Lynnea Piper argues that the creature represents the Inuits, the 'missing presence' of indigenous people during Walton's Arctic expedition. Because people recoil from him, the creature learns to hate his own appearance, seeing himself as 'a miserable deformity' who will never be accepted by human beings.

By contrasting the stories of Elizabeth and the creature, Mary Shelley emphasizes the injustice that the creature faces simply because he looks different from the other characters. No matter how hard he tries, no matter how much he seeks love and educates himself, society will always see him as 'savage' and 'monstrous'. And so this new edition of *Frankenstein* becomes a story about what Wolfson calls the disturbing and violent consequences of 'racialized preference and value'. As the scholar Adam Potkay demonstrates, the novel has played an important role in African American literary naturalism, influencing famous works such as Richard Wright's *Native Son* (1940).

By the time she finished with her revision, Mary Shelley had written her most pessimistic book, even more so than *The Last Man*, as at least Lionel undergoes a redemptive transformation. By weakening Elizabeth, she had sharpened the effects of male aggression. By 'racializing' Elizabeth and the creature she drew attention to the fraught debate over Britain's Slavery Abolition Act, which would finally be passed in 1833 (for all British colonies). She did retain MWS as the editor, but her voice is even more buried under the layers of the narrative.

As in *The Last Man*, this new edition of *Frankenstein* went against the grain of the optimism of the period, particularly the belief that science would ensure progress, and that civilization would improve the lives of people everywhere. But Mary Shelley had no patience with these clichés. Everywhere she looked she saw injustice, poverty, and hypocrisy. Driven by her need to expose class hatred, racism, and prejudice, she told her story with as much power as she could.

The reissuing of *Frankenstein* confirmed Mary Shelley's fame. And yet, she was still poor. In the ten years since Percy had died, Sir Timothy had never raised her allowance. The magazines paid well enough, and she earned some money from her fiction, but between her expenses and those of her son, Godwin, and the rest of her friends and family who leaned on her for financial support, she seemed to be always in debt, always struggling to make ends meet.

Chapter 6
The final work, 1835–1844

Mary Shelley's final novels may not appear similar, but they share a dual priority—one that she had been advocating for since *Valperga*, the cause of peace and the rights of women. To her, these ideals were deeply intertwined. As in her earlier works, the female characters are the ones who speak on behalf of balance, love, and harmony. However, where both Katherine Gordon and Euthanasia fail to stop men from waging war, in the last two novels, *Lodore* and *Falkner*, the female protagonists, Fanny Derham and Elizabeth Raby, both triumph over the impulses of the male characters and succeed in creating communities based on family and egalitarian ideals. In these final novels, women are valued for their strength, independence, and education, and men are valued for their ability to adapt to these new standards.

Lodore (1835)

Mary Shelley set *Lodore* during her own time, the 1830s. The novel revisits the ideas of her earlier work, extending and developing these themes in a contemporary setting. As in all of her previous novels, she explores the impact of masculine ambition on the lives of women, but this time she also grapples directly with the problem of female education, denouncing the shallowness of aristocratic English society. In setting the book in her own time period, Mary Shelley exposes issues that were relevant to her readers and to English society as a whole. Now that she was 'the most distinguished' female writer in England, she did not need to hide her reformist agenda and could elevate her radical beliefs. Accordingly, the salvation for the female characters can only begin when Lodore, the title character, dies and the women join forces.

Lodore is a ne'er-do-well man about town. Self-indulgent, poorly educated, and selfish, he fathers a child in an adulterous affair, and then marries 16-year-old Cornelia, a 'lovely girl, somewhat ignorant'. She is depicted as shallow and dedicated to pleasure and amusement. When she gives birth to a child, Ethel, she ignores her. Lodore, on the other hand, adores Ethel—too much, Mary Shelley implies—and to escape fighting a duel with his son from the adulterous affair emigrates to America, where he isolates Ethel from their neighbours, showering her with 'incessant care' and rendering her completely dependent on him. Like Mathilda, Ethel 'inspired' him with 'more than a father's fondness' and she in turn 'seldom thought and never acted for herself'.

When Lodore dies at the end of the first volume, his death creates a hole in the plot, undercutting the reader's expectations that a novel must revolve around a central male character. Who will step into Lodore's shoes? In Mary Shelley's hands, it is the female characters who fill the void, for once Lodore is gone the women can now take centre stage. The male characters are so weak that the women must save one another from harm and find happiness without any hope of rescue from a man. Even Edward Villier, Ethel's love interest, cannot help her out of her predicaments. In the world of *Lodore*, as in all of Mary Shelley's novels, there are no heroes.

At the age of 16, Ethel is released from her father's oppressive love and is able to move forward, establishing a positive relationship with her mother and a friendship with another young woman, Fanny Derham, an intellectual who has educated herself according to Wollstonecraft's principles. Ultimately, it is Fanny who becomes a guide for Ethel, exemplifying the values of independence and integrity.

That Mary Shelley named her heroine Fanny is a poignant tribute to her sister. In the world of the novel, Fanny lives the life Mary Shelley wished her own Fanny could have had. Self-sufficient, free of the strictures of husband and father, and supported by her female friends, Fanny Derham lives with admirable rectitude. She dedicates herself to improving the world, educating herself, helping and advising her friends, and working toward reforming society, embodying the Wollstonecraft axiom: provide women with education and freedom and the world will be a better place for everyone. At the novel's end, Fanny and Ethel join together to create the peaceful 'sentimental community' that Mary Shelley had first dreamed of in 1814.

By advancing her mother's ideas and asserting the benefits of independence for women, *Lodore* became Mary Shelley's most overtly radical book to date. She displaced the male aristocrat, Lodore, with his direct opposite—Fanny Derham, an intellectual, middle-class woman, who is independent and reads philosophy, dedicating herself to cultivating her own 'genius' and that of others. As the novel's modern editor, Lisa Vargo, writes, the book is 'an imagined conversation with [Mary Shelley's] mother, a life-writing practice that allows her to speak to and through her mother's beliefs'.

Without a historical setting or dystopian world to screen the reader from her reformist agenda, it was, perhaps, a surprise to Mary Shelley that when *Lodore* was published in 1835, the reviews were more positive than those for her other books. As had happened earlier, this was because many critics misunderstood the work, describing it as a 'romance', and overlooking its message of reform. Viewing the book as a domestic novel of manners, they praised Mary Shelley for her exploration of the secrets of the human heart and neglected its politics, particularly the elevation of Fanny and the establishment of the peaceful community at the end. Perhaps because of this oversight, the novel sold briskly.

Aubrey Beauclerk

Mary Shelley had spent the years after Percy's death mourning his loss, but as an attractive young widow she had her share of suitors. In the spring of 1832, at the age of 34, she drew the attention of a handsome young radical, 31-year-old Aubrey Beauclerk, who admired her for precisely those things that scandalized other members of English society: her writing, her politics, and her outrageous past.

Aubrey courted Mary Shelley, making efforts to talk to her when they met at parties and other social gatherings. But it was not always easy to get to know her. Although she could be warm and funny with her friends, Mary Shelley tended to be quiet in the company of strangers. Those who met her for the first time were often taken aback to find that the author of the notorious *Frankenstein* was so reserved. One new friend described his astonishment at finding her 'gentle, feminine, ladylike'. Another confessed that he had thought she would be 'indiscreet and even extravagant', but was agreeably surprised to find her 'cool, quiet, feminine'. These responses reveal the stereotypes that dominated the period. People assumed that artists and writers who wrote bold, imaginative works would themselves be bold and 'masculine', making it difficult for Mary Shelley's contemporaries to reconcile the ambitious qualities of her work with her identity as a woman and a quiet one at that.

But as an up-and-coming politician, Aubrey needed a wife who would help him advance his career. He ended the affair, and married a rich young woman free from debt and scandal. For Mary Shelley, this was a terrible loss. In Aubrey, she thought she had found another Percy. He had been ardent and loving, and held

Mary Shelley

the same political views. He fought for the abolition of slavery, supported the Irish cause, and was one of the most energetic advocates of the Reform Bill that was debated in Parliament in the spring of 1833. In the wake of this loss, writing *Lodore* became a cathartic exercise. As she worked on developing the character of Fanny Derham, Mary Shelley deepened her commitment to her mother's ideals. Like Fanny, she decided, she did not need a man. What she needed were her books, her writing, her friends, and her philosophy. She would continue to advocate for a more egalitarian society, for educational reform and social justice, but she would do so as an independent woman, an unattached, self-sufficient Fanny Derham.

Biographies

While Mary Shelley was in the midst of writing *Lodore*, Dionysius Lardner, a friend of her father, invited her to compose biographical essays for *The Cabinet Cyclopedia*. This was a signal honour, since Lardner had his pick of contributors and intended to reach a wide audience. Also, he paid well. The assignment he gave her was to write essays on the literary men of Italy, Spain, Portugal, and France. She was one of the few writers he knew who had the requisite language skills, erudition, and talent to take on this challenge. Pleased to be recognized for her abilities, Mary Shelley gladly accepted Lardner's offer, becoming the only female contributor in a literary group that included luminaries such as Sir Walter Scott.

She began work in November 1833; at the same time she was working on *Lodore* and continuing to write short stories, but she had never shied away from hard work. For the next four-and-a-half years, she researched and wrote more than 50 portraits of the 'Most Eminent Literary and Scientific Men of Italy, Spain, Portugal, and France', finishing in May 1838. For many years, historians have underestimated how many of these articles she wrote, as Lardner did not always identify the authors. However, the modern consensus is that Mary Shelley wrote at least three-quarters of the 1,757-page project. She relied largely on her own translations, and the results are among her best literary efforts. Her criticisms are cogent and illuminating. She set the lives in historical and political context, and chose vivid examples to demonstrate the strengths and weaknesses of the authors' work. Her scholarship was impeccable. 'My life and reason have been saved by these Lives,' she wrote on 2 December 1834. The partial anonymity of the articles—not all were signed, and then usually just with initials—allowed her to express her opinions without fear of repercussions. In addition, writing biography released her from some of the limitations of writing fiction. Instead of having to advance a plot, she could include her own observations, views, and political philosophy, and even parts of her own story, just as she had in *Six Weeks*, albeit refracted through the lens of the great men's lives.

Always committed to revealing the experiences of women, she spent hours reading about the lives of the mothers, wives, daughters, and sisters of her subjects. Loyal sisters, female friends, wives, mistresses, and widows fill the pages of her essays. After the first stages of research, she became so engaged in these women's lives that she, once again, proposed a volume on historical female figures, but this time to Lardner, not Murray. When Lardner refused, she resorted to amplifying the lives of the women in the biographies, advocating for the inclusion of at least a few women writers, including Madame de Staël, and her old friend Isabella Baxter's heroine, Madame Roland, in the section on French writers, and drawing lines of connection between the historical figures and the present. For example, in her portrait of Montaigne, she included several paragraphs about his friend Marie de Gournay le Jars, who edited his work after he died and was 'esteemed one of the most learned and excellent ladies of the day'; and, she adds wryly, was 'honoured by the abuse of pedants, who attacked her personal appearance and her age, in revenge for her transcending even their sex in accomplishments and understanding'.

Not only did Mary Shelley's work on these biographies help her forget Aubrey, they gave her a renewed purpose as a writer. Even if she could not dedicate her essays entirely to the lives of women, as she wished, she could still celebrate the triumphs of these historical women. She could praise their courage and their principles. She could also empathize with the many challenges that they faced.

Godwin's death

In 1836, the year after *Lodore* was published, her 80-year-old father died. The funeral was a macabre affair. In his will, Godwin had written that he wanted to be buried 'as near' his first wife 'as possible'. And so, Mary Shelley, her stepmother, and 16-year-old Percy Florence watched as the gravediggers shovelled the dirt out of Wollstonecraft's grave. 'Her coffin was found uninjured,' wrote Mary Shelley, and everyone stared down in the hole where they could see 'the cloth still over it—& the plate tarnished but legible'. It was the closest she had come to her mother since she was a few days old. And now her father was gone, too.

Before he died, Godwin had asked his daughter to write his biography and edit his unfinished works for publication. Mary Shelley began dutifully enough, but soon became paralysed by the enormous scale of the task. Godwin had kept a copy of almost every letter he had ever written and had taken voluminous notes on all his reading. There were piles of manuscripts, old drafts of many of his books, and an unpublished book critiquing organized religion. Despite the difficulty of the project, she worked on it steadily for almost four years before stopping, exhausted at the sheer effort involved. Her own work was suffering. She knew that a biography of her father would not sell well and that his diatribe against religion would harm, not help, his reputation, and so she gave up, sure that once again she had disappointed her father, but she had reached the limits of her strength.

Falkner (1837)

Although Mary Shelley could not write Godwin's biography, she still had the energy to write one more novel. The year after her father died, when she was 40, she finished *Falkner*. She thought this book was her best, but this assessment is difficult for modern readers to share as the dialogue is stiff and the characters are somewhat two dimensional. But Mary Shelley did not judge her books for their 'realistic' qualities. She cared about politics, philosophy, and human rights, and judged her books, and all books for that matter, on their ethical standards. If one adheres to these criteria, then Mary Shelley is right; *Falkner* is her best work, as it is in this novel that she gives full voice to many of her most radical ideas and the female characters enjoy their greatest triumphs.

Elizabeth, the heroine of *Falkner*, shares the same name as Frankenstein's bride, but she has far more independence and strength than the Elizabeth of either the 1818 or 1831 version. In *Frankenstein*, Mary Shelley had created a helpless victim, a symbol of feminine dependence and passivity. In the 1831 edition, she had also created a 'racialized' Elizabeth who serves as a foil to the creature. In *Falkner*, this new, improved Elizabeth is neither racialized nor weak. She conquers her enemies and redeems the men in her life, saving them from failure and disastrous fates. At the end of the novel, she helps establish the most fully realized of Mary Shelley's 'sentimental communities'.

Elizabeth is only 6 years old when she first meets John Rupert Falkner. They encounter each other in a graveyard, not unlike the graveyard where Mary Shelley and Percy first consummated their love, and where Wollstonecraft and Godwin were buried. Falkner is about to commit suicide, but the child Elizabeth saves him by crying out, distracting him from his purpose, and demonstrating her ability to take charge of an unstable situation and save an adult from himself.

Elizabeth is an orphan and so Falkner adopts her, grooming her to be as dependent on him as Ethel was on Lodore, and as the 1831 Elizabeth was on the Frankenstein family. But Elizabeth has already shown herself to be far stronger than either of *Frankenstein*'s Elizabeths, far more independent than Ethel, and wiser than the self-destructive Falkner. Accordingly, she resists his attempts to make her dependent on him, devoting herself to her studies with the help of her governess, a Wollstonecraft figure. When she is 13, Falkner (like Byron, and Raymond in *The Last Man*) goes off to fight for Greek independence, leaving Elizabeth alone at home to continue reading philosophy and literature. Like Mary Shelley's other great heroines, Euthanasia and Fanny Derham, and like Mary Shelley herself, she continues her rigorous schedule of study, reading the great works of classical philosophy and English literature, and building up her reserves of self-reliance and independence. When Falkner is wounded, she travels to Greece to rescue him, demonstrating a 'reliance on her own powers' that others admire, and also demonstrating a heroic ability to succeed where the ostensible heroes, Falkner, Byron, and Raymond, have all failed. Unlike these men, not only does she survive the battlefield, but she rescues her 'father', reversing the roles of daughter and parent by committing a trespass of the highest order. Like Katherine Gordon and Euthanasia, she ventures onto the battlefield, leaving the private sphere and entering the world of men, going against everything a woman was supposed to do.

Thanks to her courage, self-discipline, and the support of her Wollstonecraft-like governess, Elizabeth has learned to subvert the rules that bind young women of the era, refusing to become a 'timid, homebred young lady'. With each new challenge, she revolts against 'frivolous rules' and resists 'fictitious notions of propriety and false delicacy'. When Falkner is falsely accused of murder, she advocates for him, yet again saving his life while also demonstrating her independence, as others scorn her for defending a criminal. She seeks 'a bold and dangerous freedom', having been educated 'beyond the narrow paling of boarding school ideas or the refinement of a lady's boudoir'. Ultimately, she becomes braver, bolder, and more successful than any of Mary Shelley's previous heroines. She is also far more heroic than any of Mary Shelley's male characters or, for that matter, any of the men whom Mary Shelley knew in her own life.

At the end of the novel, Elizabeth marries Falkner's enemy, the man who accused him of murder. To do so, she must overcome Falkner's resistance to her love affair, but she does this with aplomb, reconciling the two men, and connecting them as part of a loving family, creating yet another one of Mary Shelley's sentimental communities. Falkner, like Lodore, and Mathilda's father, has tried to control his daughter, but Elizabeth overcomes his authoritarian impulses, as education has given her independence and the ability to think for herself. Driven by 'her love of truth', she, like Fanny Derham, is able to defy the hypocrisies of her world and convert others to a more 'philosophical' way of life. In testimony to her influence, Falkner no longer seeks to be a hero, but delights in his new capacity for 'tender' feelings and the gentleness in his soul that he now experiences. Like Lionel in *The Last Man*, he acknowledges his transformation in gendered terms, declaring that 'his man's heart' has become tender, his heart 'soft as a woman's'. Falkner's celebration of his new 'softness' reveals how Mary Shelley has turned 19th-century values upside down. In her novels, 'softness' is more of a 'virtue' than 'hardness', a tender heart more virtuous than a ruthless one—an irony, since as a well-trained classicist she knew that *virtue* came from the Latin word for man, *vir*.

Although *Falkner* received some favourable reviews, critics focused on it as a love story, overlooking the contemporary issues that Mary Shelley raised. Once again, she had used fiction to subvert and critique the values of her time, and once again this critique went largely unnoticed. For example, when Falkner is imprisoned, she provided a disquisition on the injustice of the legal system. She also included commentary on the evils of class prejudice, the problems with educational institutions, for both men and women, and even the racist policies of the British government toward India. Instead of creating male characters who save the women in their lives, she created a female character who saves her 'father' and her lover. Instead of painting war as a glorious and heroic endeavour, she demonstrated the sufferings it caused. In her hands, domestic life is transformed from being simply the province of women, a place of dull mediocrity, to the locus of community, the place where people can find 'fellow feeling with the oppressed'. Indeed, this is perhaps the most radical point of all: in the world of *Falkner*, the 'domestic sphere' is no longer the private sphere of womanhood but is instead a shared public space of harmony and virtue.

Sales of *Falkner* were slow and Mary Shelley, who was in the midst of writing the section on Spanish and Portuguese writers for Lardner, which she finished that summer, decided that *Falkner* would be her last novel. Her work as a fiction writer had come full circle. In *Frankenstein*, Victor's ambition destroys everyone he loves. Innocent people are killed, their houses burned. Margaret Saville Walton does rescue her brother, but her presence is offstage and her voice heard only indirectly; furthermore, Walton's rescue is overshadowed by the destruction caused by Victor and his creature. In *Falkner*, Mary Shelley creates a heroine who can save the male characters from ruin, preserving their lives, freeing them from destruction, and bringing them into the peace and warmth of a community. These were the goals of Euthanasia and Katherine Gordon, but they could not prevent the men in their lives from seeking after false glory. Acting as an advocate for peace, Elizabeth creates a utopian community in which men and women alike share the bounties of their life together. Without the follies generated by male ambition, Mary Shelley argues that there would be no more war and no more children lost. It was a fitting place for this reform-minded, radical writer to end her career as a novelist. But it was also a fitting place for Mary Shelley, a 40-year-old woman, to finish. Whether she was aware of it or not, in fiction she had at last recouped her losses and redeemed the suffering she had endured with Percy. In her final novel, the heroine succeeds where she, Mary Shelley, had failed. Elizabeth Raby stops the men she loves from pursuing their follies, persuading them to live with her in harmony and peace—the kind of harmony that Mary Shelley had yearned for her entire life.

Percy's *Complete Works*

In the summer of 1838, just before Mary Shelley turned 41, the distinguished publisher Edward Moxon offered her £500 to edit a four-volume set of Percy's collected poetry and prose. Moxon had published Tennyson's work and was enthusiastic about Percy's *Posthumous Poems*. He wanted Mary Shelley to overturn Sir Timothy's prohibition and compile all of Percy's work into a complete edition. He also asked her to provide a biographical background for those readers who had already encountered Percy's poems and wanted to know more about him. This was an opportunity to establish Percy's literary legacy that Mary Shelley did not want to miss. She had dreamed of bringing his work into the world since Percy had died, but she doubted that Sir Timothy would allow the project to move forward. However, the matter had become urgent, as, over the last few years, several pirated copies of Percy's poems had been published and Mary Shelley was disturbed by the many errors. She wanted to correct these mistakes and bring out a well-edited comprehensive edition of his work.

Fortunately, Sir Timothy had a new young lawyer who admired Percy's poetry and persuaded Sir Timothy to give his permission. Sir Timothy agreed, but he drew the line at a biography. He did not want the old scandals brought back into the public's memory. It had taken 16 years to rehabilitate the Shelley name. Although Sir Timothy did not give her credit for this, Mary Shelley's preface to *Posthumous Poems* had helped, but so also had the passage of time.

Frustrated though she was that Sir Timothy would not let her write her husband's life, Mary Shelley was pleased to have the chance to publish Percy's essays and poetry and she devised a strategy that would allow her to include biographical material without Sir Timothy noticing. She would write 'notes', setting Percy's writing in context, but also telling the reader details about his life. She knew this was breaking the rules, but she had learned to think strategically after all these years, and so she did it under the guise of an 'editor', not a biographer.

However, she had not realized how painful it would be to revisit the past. When she reread the old diaries and papers, she had to relive all the sorrows of that time: the loss of little Clara, Wilmouse, Fanny, and Byron. There were also happier memories—Geneva, the early years in England, the first year in Italy—but even these were difficult to bear. Most disheartening of all, though, was, once again, facing the pain they had caused Percy's first wife, Harriet. In her diary, Mary Shelley wrote, 'Poor Harriet, to whose sad fate I attribute so many of my own heavy sorrows as the atonement claimed by fate.'

Then there was the problem of the controversial work. Some of the poems promoted radical politics. Some were dedicated to other women and she was not sure how to handle this information. Should she reveal his affairs, risking Percy's reputation? After much thought, she decided to guard their privacy. A veteran of scandals, she knew that if readers knew too much they would be outraged and discount the genius of his work. When Wollstonecraft had died, Godwin's tell-all memoir had so scandalized the public that Wollstonecraft's books went out of print and those who had once admired her turned their backs on her, trying to distance themselves from her sexual escapades. Mary Shelley was not going to do this to Percy. She wanted to create a literary legacy for him, not divulge the scandals of their personal life, and so she decided the most honourable thing to do would be to tell the reader that she was leaving out some events.

She would share stories that would help them understand his work, but she would withhold others: 'This is not the time to relate the truth,' she wrote in the preface, 'and I should reject any colouring of the truth.' With this gesture, she made two points clear: there were secrets and she was not going to reveal these secrets, not because she did not want to, but because it was the wrong time—an aspersion against the prejudices of the era.

However, Mary Shelley did allow herself to relate vivid tales about their life together, describing where Percy wrote his poems, and what else was happening in their lives at the time. She captures him reading on his boat and remembers how he marvelled at fireflies. She depicts his excitement when he saw the bird that would inspire his famous poem 'To a Skylark'. She emphasizes Percy's lyricism and the purity of his convictions—how little he sought worldly fame or money, how passionately he loved his art. Mary Shelley knew that if she wanted the public to admire her husband as a poet, she must avoid mentioning his radical ideas. She was also well aware that any controversy surrounding his name would hurt her career, as well. Both of their literary legacies depended on how carefully she retold the past.

The first volume took her almost a year, during which time she became ill. In her journal, she wrote, 'I am torn to pieces by Memory.' When the reviews came, the critics praised Percy but criticized Mary Shelley. The *Spectator* and the *Athenaeum* thought her editing was awkward, and that she had left too much out. The *Examiner* disagreed with her assessments of Percy's work. Trelawny, intent on publishing his own memoirs, and seeing an opportunity to hurt Mary Shelley and advance his own career, joined the chorus of critics. Complaining that she was too deferential to Sir Timothy, he called her a coward, claiming that all she cared about was her allowance from the Shelley estate.

Trelawny's criticisms hurt, but Mary Shelley ignored them. She wanted people to read Percy's work. She needed to protect Percy

Florence. She also needed to continue to earn money to support her family. But she did decide to respond to the remarks from the literary journals, revising the first volume to include Percy's more radical essays and poems. However, as she had predicted, there was a swift reaction from conservatives. These readers sued Moxon for blasphemy, the last case of its kind in England. The conservatives lost the case; the book stayed in print, but the experience took a toll on Mary Shelley, reminding her of what she stood to lose.

Worried about what the public would say about his other, even more inflammatory work, she spent the rest of the year working on the prose volumes. She did not want 'to mutilate' Percy's ideas, she wrote to her friend Leigh Hunt, and yet she knew some of his ideas were too outrageous for readers to handle. Wisely, she did not publish those letters to her father in which Percy extols the principles of free love and argues on behalf of their illicit relationship. She also left out passages that were overtly atheistic. But when one friend suggested that she delete the homosexual references in Percy's translation of Plato's *Symposium*, she took a stand, saying it was important to keep 'As many of Shelley's own words as possible'. Labouring to make the choices that were best for her husband's legacy, she finished in 1840, exhausted and discouraged, writing in her diary that she felt as though she could never write another word.

In the preface, she apologized for any weaknesses, never realizing that her edition of Shelley's complete works would be one of the great achievements of her life. She had single-handedly brought him into the public arena, praising his poetry when few people had heard of him. Experienced fiction writer that she was, she knew how to depict Percy as a figure who would appeal to the public. She went even further than she had in 1824, in *Posthumous Poems*, telling readers that he dwelt in a higher sphere, like an angel, that he was an 'exalted being', and 'pure-minded', completing her transformation of the atheistic, anti-authoritarian

Percy into a Victorian martyr who died for the cause of liberty and virtue.

To the modern reader, Mary Shelley's portrait of Percy may seem untruthful at worst, and incomplete at best, but she had only expunged what she felt the public could not understand. To her, what was most important was his work, not the details of his life. She believed she had captured what was most important about Percy—his commitment to art and philosophy, which was, to her, the epitome of virtue. If she had told the whole truth about their life together, 19th-century readers would never have read his work and it might have been lost forever. A sell-out, Trelawny complained, but Mary Shelley was a veteran of the literary marketplace; she knew what her audience would like and what they would hate.

Complete Works was a sensation. New readers praised his lyrical genius. The old scandals faded away. Before long, Percy was celebrated as one of the great English poets, having gone from being a renegade to 'Christian-hearted', from being a scandal-ridden cad to a literary star. Mary Shelley had done her job so skilfully that no one bothered to dig below the surface.

In part, this was due to the fact that she had become a master of invisibility, leaving behind only traces of her presence. Like Margaret Walton Saville, or 'the editor' of *The Last Man* or *Valperga*, she fades into the background, never revealing the effort she has poured into recreating his work. Instead, she lets him take centre stage, as though he is one of her literary creations, like Lionel Verney, or one of her female heroines, Fanny Derham, or Elizabeth Raby. When pressed, Mary Shelley declared that she was fortunate to have lived with such a noble soul whose dedication to love and purity was truly remarkable. She was nothing next to him, she declared. And so, in the end, she created another character, one of the most long-lasting of all her creations, a fictional Mary Shelley, a Victorian wife and humble scribe. Like

Victor Frankenstein's creature, this 'Mary Shelley' was the invention of a master novelist, and was as different from the actual Mary Shelley as 'Shelley the poet' was from the real Percy.

As she worked on promoting Percy's reputation, her own fame continued to grow. In the winter of 1839, her friend Richard Rothwell painted her portrait for the Royal Academy (Figure 8). In the painting, she wears a low-cut black dress. Her hair is tidy

8. **Mary Shelley by Richard Rothwell (1839).**

and her face pale. She looks beautiful, melancholy, and worn down, as indeed she was—too weary to hide her sadness from the artist.

Rambles in Germany and Italy, in 1840, 1842, and 1843 (1844)

Despite her exhaustion, at the age of 42 Mary Shelley decided that the time had finally come to return to Europe. After years of living frugally, she had saved enough money for this trip, and she, Percy Florence, and one of his Cambridge friends set forth for Italy in June 1840, visiting many of the old sites. She enjoyed herself so much that, two years later, they returned to Europe, this time to spend more time in Venice and Rome. Her joy at these returns was tinged with sorrow. She tried to find the graves of Clara and William, but they were unmarked. She also visited Percy's grave in the Protestant cemetery in Rome.

When they returned to England, after their last trip abroad, Mary Shelley organized the notes she had taken and by January 1844 had finished the first volume of what would be her last work, a travel book she titled *Rambles in Germany and Italy*. Like her first book, *Six Weeks*, and, indeed, all of her books, *Rambles* was a tribute for her mother, but it was also a fitting end to her own career. As in *Six Weeks*, she praises the sublime qualities of nature, and delves into politics, exposing the evils of Austria's occupation of Italy. She analyses the art she sees, revealing her acuity as a critic, and also refers to ideas from *The Symposium* that she had once helped Percy translate. Artists should not be vilified for depicting scenes of homosexual love, she wrote—a stance that could have earned her a sharp rebuke if any of the critics had noticed it. But once again reviewers overlooked her critical theories and her politics. No one noted her endorsement of homosexuality, her erudition, or her observations on art. Some reviewers enjoyed the charm of the narrative, and a few did applaud her anti-Austrian stance, as this was a popular foreign policy. But Mary Shelley was not unduly cast down. For her, there was nothing new about being misunderstood. Even if the reviewers didn't realize it, she knew she had triumphed in the end. An independent and self-sufficient woman, she had published all of her books under her own name, filling them with her own thoughts and ideas, her radical politics, and her cultural criticism—a long journey from 1817, when she had been dependent on her lover to support her, had published her first books anonymously and endured social exile for being an unmarried mother. Now, she was an author who had successfully raised a son and supported friends and family for most of her adult life.

Final years

In 1844, Sir Timothy died, giving Mary Shelley and her son their first taste of financial security. At long last, the Shelley ancestral home in Sussex belonged to 23-year-old Percy Florence. Mary Shelley was relieved, but she had begun to feel ill during their travels in Italy, and grew steadily worse over the next few years. She worried about Percy, hoping to see him happily married before she died. One of her concerns was that he would choose the wrong person, someone who would take advantage of his trusting nature. Fortunately, in 1848, he married a young woman named Jane, who was sensible, loyal, and, best of all, devoted to her mother-in-law. For the next three years, Mary Shelley lived with the young couple, growing weaker until she died on 1 February 1851, at the age of 53. In the last month of her life, she lost the power to speak and her left leg was paralysed. The final diagnosis was a brain tumour. Jane and Percy Florence were at her bedside when 'her sweet gentle spirit passed away', as Jane later recalled in a letter to her friend Alexander Berry on 7 March 1851. Percy was devastated. He had always lived with his mother, except for his years at university. Together, they had carved out a life, filled with beauty, contentment, and good friends. Now, he felt lost, without a centre. Fortunately, Jane helped him heal, encouraging him to follow his favourite pastimes—sailing and amateur theatre.

In the years after her mother-in-law's death, Jane swept into action, taking steps that still appal biographers and historians. She wanted Mary Shelley to be seen as a pious, grieving widow, not as a rebellious young woman who lived with a man out of wedlock and had three illegitimate children. To cover up her mother-in-law's history, she went through Mary Shelley's papers, burning letters and ripping pages out of diaries. She also wrote her own untruthful version of Mary and Percy's courtship in a book she entitled *Shelley Memorials*. Published in 1859, this volume was designed to clear the family of all scandals. Declaring that Mary Shelley had told her the real story of her relationship with Percy, Jane wrote that the young lovers had only confessed their feelings after Harriet had died. She also said that it was Percy who initiated their love affair, not Mary Shelley.

Jane's efforts were so successful that it took over a century for the truth to re-emerge. Just as Mary Shelley had created an angelic personage, the ideal Victorian poet, in place of the real Percy Shelley, so Jane created a selfless wife and daughter, an ideal Victorian woman, in place of the impassioned 16-year-old, the outrageous daughter of Wollstonecraft, who declared her love for a married man and ran away with him to Paris. Mary Shelley's self-deprecation, her portrait of herself as nothing more than a devoted wife, and her silence about their life together in the volumes she published of Percy's work, supported these portraits as did the obituaries that came out after her death.

Jane and Percy Florence moved from Field Place to Bournemouth on the south coast of England, buying a large estate called Boscombe Manor. Here, Jane promoted the image of Mary Shelley as the docile wife of the great poet, building a shrine to her mother-in-law (Figure 9). She draped a corner of her drawing room in red velvet and painted the ceiling blue with yellow dots for stars. She hung the Rothwell portrait of Mary Shelley on the wall behind a row of glass covered cases that contained precious items, such as Mary Shelley's hand mirror and Mary

9. Percy and Mary Shelley's locks of hair, preserved in a locket.

Wollstonecraft's amethyst ring. The pièce de résistance was an urn containing the remains of Percy's heart, which his son had found a year after Mary Shelley died. He had been too grief-stricken to unlock his mother's writing desk immediately after her death, but when at last he did, he discovered her journal, a folded copy of one of Percy's poems, *Adonais*, and inside the paper, the dusty remains of his father's heart.

Generally speaking, Victorian society embraced this image of Mary Shelley as a paragon of virtue, but the vindictive Trelawny capitalized on this false portrait of Mary Shelley to further his claims that she was a hypocrite, painting the Shelleys' marriage as a disaster in his self-promoting account of Percy Shelley's life, *Records of Shelley, Byron, and the Author* (1878).

For over a century, Mary Shelley, the woman who had begun her public life as a renegade and a rule-breaker, would be known as a pious wife or a hypocrite, depending on the point of view of the writer. She would be condemned for many contradictory failings, compromising the radical values of her husband or failing him with her mediocre views. Gradually, people forgot that she was the daughter of the famous radical Mary Wollstonecraft. If people knew her at all, it was as the author of *Frankenstein* and many doubted that she wrote even that, as some held that Percy must have been the author.

However, her last public act demonstrated her commitment to women's independence and her mother's values, invisible though it was to the outside world. A few months before Mary Shelley died, Isabella (Baxter) Booth, her old friend from Scotland, wrote to ask if Mary Shelley would petition the Royal Literary Fund for assistance on her behalf. Mary Shelley had not heard from Isabella in years, as Isabella's husband, David Booth, had not allowed Isabella to be in touch with her friend after Mary Shelley ran away with Percy. But now, having nursed her writer husband through a long illness, Isabella was penniless and desperate. Despite the rupture in their friendship that had left her heartbroken, Mary Shelley, near death, hardly able to pen a legible word, knew what it was like to have no money. She wrote to the Fund on 15 November 1850, connecting Isabella's plight to the sufferings of all women. 'Her husband's malady demanded a care and courage in nursing,' she wrote, 'which for a woman to undertake and go through alone demanded heroic exertion.'

Heroic exertion. These words resonate in part because they are the last she ever wrote, but also because they could be said of Mary Shelley herself. Like Isabella, it had taken 'heroic exertion' to overcome the challenges she faced: she had written nine books, more than 50 stories, articles, and biographical sketches supporting herself and those who depended on her in a world that

10. Idealized portrait of Mary Shelley as a young widow. Painted posthumously, this image is based on recollections of her son and daughter-in-law, as well as a death mask.

condemned her for the choices she had made as a 16-year-old girl and also condemned her mother.

The Fund rejected her petition, but Mary Shelley did not want Isabella to suffer and, in her will, asked Percy to send her old friend an allowance of £50 a year—a symbol of her dedication to improving the lives of women. In her novels, essays, and stories, and in her quiet behind-the-scenes actions, Mary Shelley had made the plight of women the driving force of her life. And yet, this truth was almost lost to history. It is only now, with access to her journals, letters, and diaries, as well as the important critical studies of the last few decades, that she is recognized for her courage and her creativity, her authorial innovations and her struggles. To the end of her days, she tried to live by the words of her mother, Mary Wollstonecraft, seeking to reform the world by vindicating the rights of women (Figure 10).

Further reading

Mary Shelley's letters and journals

Betty T. Bennett (ed.), *The Letters of Mary Wollstonecraft Shelley*,
   3 vols (Baltimore: Johns Hopkins University Press, 1980–8).
Paula R. Feldman and Diana Scott-Kilvert (eds), *The Journals of
   Mary Shelley, 1814–1844* (Baltimore: Johns Hopkins University
   Press, 1987).

Collected works by Mary Shelley

Nora Crook (gen. ed.), *The Novels & Selected Works of Mary Shelley*,
   8 vols (London: Pickering & Chatto, 1996).
Betty T. Bennett and Charles Robinson (eds), *The Mary Shelley Reader*
   (Oxford: Oxford University Press, 1990).

Editions of *Frankenstein*

Charles Robinson (ed.), *Mary Shelley (with Percy Shelley)*, *The
   Original Frankenstein: Two New Versions: Mary Shelley's Earliest
   Draft and Percy Shelley's Revised Text* (New York: Vintage, 2011).
Charles Robinson (ed.), *The Frankenstein Notebooks*, 2 vols (New
   York: Routledge, 1996).
Mary Shelley, *Frankenstein: The 1818 Text* (reprint, New York:
   Penguin, 2018).
Mary Shelley, *Mary Shelley's Frankenstein (1831). Norton Critical
   Edition* (New York: W. W. Norton, 1996).

Other selected individual works

Mary Shelley, *A History of a Six Weeks Tour Through a Part of France, Switzerland, and Holland* (London: T. Hookham, and C. and J. Ollier, 1817). Available online: <https://www.google.com/books/edition/History_of_a_Six_Weeks_Tour_Through_a_Pa/u1YJAAAAQAAJ?hl=en&gbpv=0>.

Lisa Vargo (ed.), *Lodore* (London: 1833; Ontario: Broadview Press, 1997).

Janet Todd (ed.), *Matilda* in *Mary Wollstonecraft: Mary and Maria; Mary Shelley: Matilda* (London: Penguin Classics, 1992).

Mary Shelley, *The Last Man* (Oxford: Oxford University Press, 1998), introduction by Morton Paley.

Mary Shelley, *Valperga* (Oxford: Oxford University Press, 2000).

'Giovanni Villani', *The Mary Shelley Reader*, 329–33.

'On Ghosts', *The Mary Shelley Reader*, 334–40.

'Transformation', *The Mary Shelley Reader*, 286–300.

Mary Shelley, *The Fortunes of Perkin Warbeck* (London, 1830).

Mary Shelley (and others), *Lives of The Most Eminent French Writers* (Philadelphia: Lea and Blanchard, 1840).

Mary Shelley, *Falkner*, 3 vols (London: Saunders and Otley, 1837).

Mary Shelley (ed.), Percy Shelley, *Posthumous Poems* (London: John and Henry Hunt, 1824).

Collected critical essays

Helen M. Buss, D. L. Macdonald, and Anne McWhir (eds), *Mary Wollstonecraft and Mary Shelley: Writing Lives* (Waterloo, Ont.: Wilfrid Laurier University Press, 2001).

Syndy M. Conger, Frederick S. Frank, and Gregory O'Dea (eds), *Iconoclastic Departures: Mary Shelley after Frankenstein* (Madison: University of Wisconsin Press, 1997).

Michael Eberle-Sinatra and Nora Crook (eds), *Mary Shelley's Fictions: From Frankenstein to Falkner* (New York: Macmillan, 2000).

Audrey Fisch, Anne K. Mellor, and Esther H. Schor (eds), *The Other Mary Shelley: Beyond Frankenstein* (Oxford: Oxford University Press, 1993).

Esther Schor (ed.), *The Cambridge Companion to Mary Shelley* (Cambridge: Cambridge University Press, 2003).

Biographies and group studies

Betty T. Bennett, *Mary Wollstonecraft Shelley: An Introduction* (Baltimore: Johns Hopkins University Press, 1994).

Betty T. Bennett and Stuart Curran, *Mary Shelley in Her Times* (Baltimore: Johns Hopkins Press, 2000).

Charlotte Gordon, *Romantic Outlaws: The Lives of Mary Wollstonecraft and Mary Shelley* (New York: Random House, 2015).

Daisy Hay, *Young Romantics: The Tangled Lives of English Poetry's Greatest Generation* (New York: Farrar, Straus and Giroux, 2010).

William St Clair, *The Godwins and the Shelleys* (London: Faber, 1989).

Miranda Seymour, *Mary Shelley* (New York: Grove/Atlantic, 2000).

Fiona Simpson, *In Search of Mary Shelley: The Girl Who Wrote Frankenstein* (London: Pegasus Books, 2018).

Emily Sunstein, *Mary Shelley: Romance and Reality* (Baltimore: Johns Hopkins University Press, 1989).

Angela Wright, *Mary Shelley* (Cardiff: University of Wales Press, 2018).

Chapter 1: Legacies

Athenaeum, 15 February 1851, no. 1216, p. 191.

Betty T. Bennett, 'Finding Mary Shelley in Her Letters', in *Romantic Revisions*, ed. Robert Brinkley and Keith Hanley (Cambridge: Cambridge University Press, 1992).

Betty T. Bennett, 'Mary Shelley's Letters: The Public/Private Self', in *The Cambridge Companion*.

Eileen Hunt Botting, 'From Revolutionary Paris to Nootka Sound to Saint-Domingue: The International Politics and Prejudice behind Wollstonecraft's Theory of the Rights of Humanity, 1789–91', *Journal of International Political Theory* (2020): 1–20.

Julie Carlson, *England's First Family of Writers: Mary Wollstonecraft, William Godwin, Mary Shelley* (Baltimore: Johns Hopkins Press, 2007).

Ranita Chatterjee, 'Filial Ties: Godwin's *Deloraine* and Mary Shelley's Writings', *European Romantic Reviews* 18 no. 1 (2007): 29–41. Taylor and Francis Online.

Pamela Clemit and Gina Luria Walker (eds), William Godwin, *Memoirs of the Author of a Vindication of the Rights of Woman*,

Broadview Literary Texts (Peterborough, Ont.: Broadview Press, 2001).

E. J. Clery, 'Mary Wollstonecraft: A Feminist Exile in Paris', *Litteraria Pragensia* 29 no. 57 (2019) <http://litteraria-pragensia.ff.cuni.cz/front.issue/detail/59>.

William Godwin, *Memoirs of the Author of a Vindication of the Rights of Woman*, 2nd edn (London, 1798).

Charlotte Gordon, *Romantic Outlaws: The Lives of Mary Wollstonecraft and Mary Shelley* (New York: Random House, 2015).

Richard Holmes, *The Pursuit* (New York: New York Review Books, 1994).

Claudia Johnson, 'Introduction', in *The Cambridge Companion*, 1–5.

Cora Kaplan, 'Mary Wollstonecraft's Reception and Legacies', in *The Cambridge Companion*, 246–70.

Anne Mellor, *Mary Shelley: Her Life, Her Fiction, Her Monsters* (New York: Routledge, 1988).

Mitzi Myers, 'Mary Wollstonecraft Shelley: The Female Author between Public and Private Spheres', in *Mary Shelley in Her Times*.

Victoria Myers, David O'Shaughnessy, and Mark Philp (eds), *The Diary of William Godwin* (Oxford: Oxford Digital Library, 2010) <http://godwindiary.bodleian.ox.ac.uk>.

On 'Prostitution', Miranda Seymour, *Mary Shelley*. See also *European Magazine*, April 1798 (33: 246–51).

Mary Poovey, *The Proper Lady and the Woman Writer: Ideology as Style in the Works of Mary Wollstonecraft, Mary Shelley, and Jane Austen* (Chicago: University of Chicago Press, 1984).

Miranda Seymour, *Mary Shelley* (New York: Grove/Atlantic, 2000).

Mary Shelley, 'Preface', *Complete Poetical Works of Percy Bysshe Shelley*, 2 vols, ed. Thomas Hutchinson (Oxford: Oxford University Press, 1914).

'Mary Shelley's Obituary', *The Literary Gazette*, 22 February 1851.

Muriel Spark, *Child of Light: A Reassessment of Mary Wollstonecraft Shelley* (Hadleigh: Tower Bridge, 1951). Expanded edition published as *Mary Shelley* (London: Carcanet, 2013).

Edward Trelawny, *Records of Shelley, Byron and the Author* (London, 1878). Also, *Letters of Edward John Trelawny*, ed. Henry Buxton Forman (London: Henry Frowde, Oxford University Press, 1910).

Janet Todd (ed.), Mary Wollstonecraft, *The Collected Letters of Mary Wollstonecraft* (New York: Columbia University Press, 2003).

Mary Shelley's portrait of a father and daughter can be found in 'The Elder Son', *Mary Shelley: Collected Tales and Stories*, ed. Charles E. Robinson (Baltimore: Johns Hopkins University Press, 1976).

Chapter 2: Gothic rebellion

Pamela Clemit and A. A. Markley (eds), *Life of William Godwin, Poems, Translations, Uncollected Prose*, Volume 4 of *Mary Shelley's Literary Lives and Other Writings*, gen. ed. Nora Crook, 4 vols, Pickering Masters Series (London: Pickering & Chatto, 2002), pp. xiii–xxvii, 1–381.

E. J. Clery, *Women's Gothic: From Clara Reeve to Mary Shelley* (Horndon: Northcote House Publishers Ltd, 2000 and 2004).

Ernest Hartley Coleridge (ed.), *Letters of Samuel Taylor Coleridge*, 2 vols (Boston: Houghton Mifflin, 1895).

William Godwin, *An Enquiry Concerning Political Justice and Its Influence on Morals*, 2 vols (London: Robinson, 1798).

Thomas Hogg, *The Life of Percy Bysshe Shelley* (London, 1858).

'Harriet Shelley to Catherine Nugent', ? October 1814, quoted in Seymour, *Mary Shelley*.

Anne Mellor and Noelle Chao (eds), *Mary Wollstonecraft, 'A Vindication of the Rights of Woman' and 'The Wrongs of Woman; or Maria'* (London: Pearson, 2007).

Mary Wollstonecraft Shelley, 'Life of Shelley' (1823), Bodleian, facsimile and transcript ed. A. M. Weinberg, Bodleian Shelley Manuscripts, 22 pt 2 (1997), 266–7.

Mary Wollstonecraft, 'Unfortunate Situation of Females, Fashionably Educated, and Left Without a Fortune', in *Thoughts on the Education of Daughters, with Reflections on Female Conduct* (London: J. Johnson, 1788), 69–78.

Dorothy Wordsworth, *Recollections of a Tour Made in Scotland, 1803*, ed. Carol Kyros Walker (New Haven: Yale University Press, 1997).

Angela Wright, *Gothic Fiction* (New York: Palgrave Macmillan, 2007).

Angela Wright, *Mary Shelley* (Cardiff: University of Wales Press, 2018).

Chapter 3: *Frankenstein*

Patrick Brantlinger, 'The Reading Monster', reprinted in Mary Shelley's *Frankenstein*, Norton Critical Edition (New York: W. W. Norton, 1996).

Marilyn Butler, 'The First *Frankenstein* and Radical Science', *Times Literary Supplement*, 1 Jan. 1993, reprinted in Mary Shelley's *Frankenstein*, Norton Critical Edition (New York: W. W. Norton, 1996).

'Frankenstein; or the Modern Prometheus', *The Literary Panorama*, vol. 8, April 1818.

Jane Goodall, 'Electrical Romanticism', reprinted in Mary Shelley's *Frankenstein*, Norton Critical Edition (New York: W. W. Norton, 1996).

Anne Mellor, 'Making a Monster: An Introduction to *Frankenstein*', in *The Cambridge Companion*.

Anna Mercer, *The Collaborative Literary Relationship of Percy Bysshe Shelley and Mary Wollstonecraft Shelley* (New York: Routledge, 2019).

'Review of *Frankenstein*', *The Scots Magazine and Edinburgh Literary Miscellany*, 81 (Edinburgh: Archibald Constable & Co., 1818).

James O'Rourke, 'Nothing More Unnatural: Mary Shelley's Revision of Rousseau', *English Literary History* 56 no. 3 (1989): 543–69.

Adam Potkay, '*Frankenstein* in the History of Happiness: From Ancient Ethics to Richard Wright', *The Keats-Shelley Review* 34 no. 1 (2020): 35–45. DOI: 10.1080/09524142.2020.1761113.

Charles E. Robinson, 'A Mother's Daughter: An Intersection of Mary Shelley's *Frankenstein* and Mary Wollstonecraft's *A Vindication of the Rights of Woman*', in *Writing Lives*.

Walter Scott, 'Remarks on *Frankenstein*', *Blackwood's Edinburgh Magazine*, March 1818.

Mary Wollstonecraft, *Letters Written During a Short Residence in Sweden, Norway, and Denmark* (London: J. Johnson, 1796*)*.

Paul Youngquist and Orrin N.C. Wang, <http://romantic-circles.org/reference/chronologies/mschronology/reviews.html>.

Chapter 4: Early female narrators: *A History of a Six Weeks Tour Through a Part of France, Switzerland, and Holland* and *Mathilda* (1817–1821)

Pamela Clemit, '*Frankenstein*, *Matilda*, and the Legacies of Godwin and Wollstonecraft', in *The Cambridge Companion*, 26–44.

Margaret Cohen, *The Sentimental Education of the Novel* (Princeton: Princeton University Press, 2018).

Benjamin Colbert, 'Contemporary Notice of the Shelleys' *History of a Six Weeks' Tour*: Two New Early Reviews', *Keats–Shelley Journal* 48 (1999): 22–9.

Jenny DiPlacidi, 'Introduction', in *Mathilda & Other Stories* (Hertfordshire: Wordsworth Editions Ltd., 2013).

Michelle Faubert, 'A Family Affair: Ennobling Suicide in Mary Shelley's *Matilda*', *Essays in Romanticism* 20 no. 7 (2013): 101–28. DOI: 10.3828/eir.2013.20.7.

Deana P. Koretsky, 'The Interracial Marriage Plot: Suicide and the Politics of Blood in Romantic-Era Women's Fiction', *Studies in the Literary Imagination* 51 no. 1 (2018): 1–18. DOI: 10.1353/sli.2018.0001.

Jeanne Moskal, 'Mary Shelley's Travel Writings', in *The Cambridge Companion*, 242–58.

Paul Stock, 'Liberty and Independence: The Shelley–Byron Circle and the State(s) of Europe', *Romanticism* 15 no. 2 (2009): 121–30. <http://eprints.lse.ac.uk/32163/1/Liberty%20and%20 Independence%20The%20Shelley%E2%80%93Byron%20 Circle%20(LSERO).pdf>.

Angela Wright, *Mary Shelley* (Cardiff: University of Wales Press, 2018).

Chapter 5: *Valperga*, *The Last Man*, *The Fortunes of Perkin Warbeck*, and the new *Frankenstein* (1821–1831)

Betty T. Bennett, *Mary Wollstonecraft Shelley: An Introduction* (Baltimore: Johns Hopkins University Press, 1994).

Betty T. Bennett, *Mary Diana Dods: A Gentleman and a Scholar* (New York: Morrow, 1991).

John Bugg, 'Teaching Frankenstein and Race', *The Keats-Shelley Review* 34 no. 1 (2020): 22–34. DOI: 10.1080/09524142.2020.1761111.

E. J. Clery, *Women's Gothic: From Clara Reeve to Mary Shelley* (Horndon: Northcote House Publishers Ltd, 2000 and 2004).

Michael Eberle-Sinatra, 'Gender Authorship and Male Domination: Mary Shelley's Limited Freedom in *Frankenstein* and *The Last Man*', in *Mary Shelley's Fictions*.

Neil Fraistat, 'Illegitimate Shelley: Radical Piracy and the Textual Edition as Cultural Performance', *PMLA* 109 no. 3 (1994).

Erin L. Webster Garret, 'The Politics of Ambivalence: Romance, History, and Gender in Mary Wollstonecraft Shelley's *Fortunes of*

Perkin Warbeck', The Free Library (Indiana University, 2007). Retrieved 21 July 2021 from <https://www.thefreelibrary.com/The+politics+of+ambivalence%3a+romance%2c+history%2c+and+gender+in+Mary+W....-a0174818260>.

Charlotte Gordon, *Romantic Outlaws: The Lives of Mary Wollstonecraft and Mary Shelley* (New York: Random House, 2015).

Barbara Johnson, 'The Last Man', in *The Other Mary Shelley*.

Maggie Kilgour, 'One Immortality: The Shaping of the Shelleys in *The Last Man*', *European Romantic Review* 16 no. 5 (2005): 563–88.

Joseph Lew, 'God's Sister: History and Ideology in *Valperga*', in *The Other Mary Shelley*.

Literary Gazette, no. 319 (1 March 1823): 132–3.

Deidre Lynch, 'Historical Novelist', in *The Cambridge Companion*.

H. L. Malchow, 'Frankenstein's Monster and Images of Race in Nineteenth-Century Britain', *Past and Present* 139 (May 1993): 90–130. http://www.jstor.org/stable/651092.

Ann Mellor, '*Frankenstein*, Racial Science, and the Yellow Peril', reprinted in Mary Shelley's *Frankenstein*. Norton Critical Edition (New York: W. W. Norton, 1996).

Ann Mellor, 'Possessing Nature: The Female in Frankenstein', reprinted in Mary Shelley's *Frankenstein*. Norton Critical Edition (New York: W. W. Norton, 1996).

Barbara Jane O'Sullivan, 'Beatrice in *Valperga*: A New Cassandra', in *The Other Mary Shelley*.

Morton Paley, 'The Last Man: Apocalypse without Millennium', in *The Other Mary Shelley*.

Morton Paley, 'Introduction', *The Last Man* (Oxford: Oxford University Press, 1998).

Karen Lynnea Piper, 'Inuit Diasporas: Frankenstein and the Inuit in England', *Romanticism* 13 no. 1 (2007): 63–75. Project MUSE muse.jhu.edu/article/214804.

Tilottama Rajan, 'Between Romance and History: Possibility and Contingency in Godwin, Leibniz, and Mary Shelley's Valperga', in *Mary Shelley in Her Times*.

Robert Reid, *The Peterloo Massacre* (London: William Heinemann. 1989).

Michael Rossington, 'The Republican Tradition and Its Destiny in *Valperga*', in *Mary Shelley in Her Times*.

Edward Trelawny, *Recollections of the Last Days of Byron and Shelley* (London: Edward Moxon, 1858).

Ann M. Frank Wake, 'Women in the Active Voice: Recovering Female History in Mary Shelley's *Valperga* and *Perkin Warbeck*', in *Iconoclastic Departures*.

Samantha Webb, 'Reading the End of the World: *The Last Man*, History and the Agency of Romantic Authorship', in *Mary Shelley in Her Times*.

Susan Wolfson, 'Introduction: *Frankenstein*, Race and Ethics', *The Keats-Shelley Review* 34 no. 1 (2020): 12–21 <https://www.tandfonline.com/doi/full/10.1080/09524142.2020.1761110 (DOI: 10.1080/09524142.2020.1761110)>.

Angela Wright, *Mary Shelley* (Cardiff: University of Wales Press, 2018).

Chapter 6: The final work, 1835–1844

Kate Ferguson Ellis, 'Falkner and Other Fictions', in *The Cambridge Companion*.

Bryn Gravitt, 'A Feminist Utopia? Revisions of Family in Mary Shelley's *Falkner*', *Parlour: A Journal of Literary Criticism and Analysis* (21 September 2016) <https://www.ohio.edu/cas/parlour/news/library/mary-shelleys-falkner>.

Gary Kelly, 'The Politics of Autobiography in Mary Wollstonecraft and Mary Shelley', in *Writing Lives*.

Greg Kucich, 'Biographer', in *The Cambridge Companion*.

Jeanne Moskal, 'Introductory Note to *Rambles*', in *The Novels and Selected Works of Mary Shelley*, vol. 8, ed. Jeanne Moskal (London: Pickering and Chatto, 1996).

Jeanne Moskal, 'Speaking the Unspeakable: Art Criticism in Shelley's *Rambles*', in *Writing Lives*.

Eliza Rennie, 'An Evening at Dr Kitchiner's', in *Friendship's Offering* (London, 1842), 2: 243–9.

Julia Saunders, 'Rehabilitating the Family in Mary Shelley's Falkner', in *Mary Shelley's Fictions*.

Miranda Seymour, *Mary Shelley* (New York: Grove/Atlantic, 2000).

Melissa Sites, 'Re/membering Home: Utopian Domesticity in Mary Shelley's *Lodore*', *A Brighter Morn: The Shelley Circle's Utopian Project*, ed. Darby Lewes (Lanham, Md: Lexington Books, 2003).

Melissa Sites, 'Utopian Domesticity as Social Reform in Mary *Shelley's Falkner*', *Keats-Shelley Journal* 54 (2005): 148–72.

Fiona Stafford, '*Lodore*: A Tale of the Present Time?', in *Mary Shelley's Fictions*.

'Mary Wollstonecraft Shelley's Obituary', *The Leader*, 1851, quoted in
    Emily Sunstein, *Mary Shelley*, 384.
Lisa Vargo, 'Further Thoughts on the Education of Daughters: *Lodore*
    as an Imagined Conversation with Mary Wollstonecraft', in
    Writing Lives.
Nicholas Williams, 'Angelic Realism: Domestic Idealization in Mary
    Shelley's *Lodore*', *Studies in the Novel* 39 no. 4 (2007): 397–415.
Susan Wolfson, 'Mary Shelley, Editor', in *The Cambridge Companion*.

Index

For the benefit of digital users, indexed terms that span two pages (e.g., 52–53) may, on occasion, appear on only one of those pages.

Mary Shelley

Mary Shelley